Learn Every Day About Seasons

Edited by Kathy Charner

Learn Every Day About SEASONS

100 BEST IDEAS from TEACHERS

EDITED BY
Kathy Charner
Illustrated by Deb Johnson

© 2011 Gryphon House, Inc.
Published by Gryphon House, Inc.
10770 Columbia Pike, Suite 201
Silver Spring, MD 20901
800.638.0928; 301.595.9500; 301.595.0051 (fax)

Visit us on the web at www.gryphonhouse.com

Illustrations: Deb Johnson

Cover Photo Credit: ©2010 iStockphoto LP. iStockphoto®, iStock®, iStockaudio®, iStockvideo®, iStockalypse™, Vetta® and CopySpace® are registered trademarks of iStockphoto LP. All other marks are the property of their respective owners. www.istockphoto.com.

LIBRARY OF CONGRESS CATALOGING-IN-PUBLICATION DATA

Learn every day about seasons / edited by Kathy Charner.
   p. cm.
 ISBN 978-0-87659-364-6 (pbk.)
1. Seasons--Study and teaching (Preschool)--Activity programs. 2. Seasons--Study and teaching (Early childhood)--Activity programs. 3. Education, Preschool--Activity programs. 4. Activity programs in education.
I. Charner, Kathy.
 QB637.4.L43 2011
 372.35'7--dc22

                2011011471

BULK PURCHASE

Gryphon House books are available for special premiums and sales promotions as well as for fund-raising use. Special editions or book excerpts also can be created to specification. For details, contact the Director of Marketing at Gryphon House.

DISCLAIMER

Gryphon House, Inc., and the author cannot be held responsible for damage, mishap, or injury incurred during the use of or because of activities in this book. Appropriate and reasonable caution and adult supervision of children involved in activities and corresponding to the age and capability of each child are recommended at all times. Do not leave children unattended at any time. Observe safety and caution at all times.

Table of Contents

Note: The books listed in the Related Children's Books section of each activity may occasionally include books that are only available used or through your local library.

Introduction

You have in your hands a great teacher resource! This book, which is part of the Learn Every Day series, contains 100 activities you can use with children ages 3–6 to help them develop a lifelong love of learning, as well as the knowledge and skills all children need to become successful in kindergarten and beyond. The activities in this book are written by teachers and professionals from the field of early childhood education—educators and professionals who use these activities in their classrooms every day.

The activities in this book are organized by curriculum areas, such as Art, Dramatic Play, Outdoor Play, Transitions, and so on, and within these categories according to their age appropriateness, so activities appropriate for children ages three and up come first, then activities for children ages four and up, and finally activities for children ages five and up. Each activity has the following components—learning objectives, a list of related vocabulary words, a list of thematically related books, a list of the materials (if any) you need to complete the activity, and directions for preparation and the activity itself. Also included in each activity is an assessment component to help you observe how well the children are meeting the learning objectives. Given the emphasis on accountability in early childhood education, these assessment strategies are essential.

Several activities also contain teacher-to-teacher tips that provide smart and useful ideas, including how to expand the central idea of an activity in a new way, or where to find the materials necessary to complete a given activity. Some activities also include related fingerplays, poems, or songs that you can sing and chant with the children. Children love singing, dancing, and chanting, actions that reinforce children's understanding of an activity's learning objectives.

This book and each of the other books in the series give early childhood educators 100 great activities that require few materials and little, if any, preparation, and are sure to make learning fun and engaging for children.

A Wreath for Every Season 3+

LEARNING OBJECTIVES

The children will:

1. Develop their small motor skills.
2. Learn about the differences between the seasons.

Materials

- card stock
- glue
- cut shapes
- cupcake papers
- Easter grass
- flower pictures
- pumpkin shapes
- foam shapes from a craft store
- pictures from magazines
- shapes from die cuts

VOCABULARY

fall	flower	grass	leaf	pumpkin
rainbow	season	shamrock	snow	snowflake
spring	summer	sun	winter	

PREPARATION

- Cut the card stock into circles, and then cut out their centers, making donut shapes to which the children can glue objects.

WHAT TO DO

1. At the start of each new season, talk with the children about what the season means to them. Ask for ideas of images and objects that they associate with the season.
2. Show the children the materials that they will be using to make seasonal wreaths.
3. Help the children sort through the images and objects and find things that they associate with the season, and then help them attach the images and objects to their wreaths.

TEACHER-TO-TEACHER TIP

- Bring the children outside so they can collect items to add to their wreaths, such as twigs, leaves, acorns, seeds, dandelions, small stones, and so on.

ASSESSMENT

To assess the children's learning, consider the following:

- Can the children distinguish between the seasons?
- Are the children able to glue and decorate their wreaths with season-appropriate images?

Sandie Nagel, White Lake, MI

Children's Books

Fall by Núria Roca
Four Seasons Make a Year by Anne Rockwell and Megan Halsey
Our Seasons by Ranida T. McKneally and Grace Lin
Spring by Núria Roca
Summer by Núria Roca
Watching the Seasons by Edana Eckart
Winter by Núria Roca

Growing with the Seasons

3+

LEARNING OBJECTIVES

The children will:
1. Learn how nature changes with the seasons.
2. Develop their artistic and small motor skills.

Materials

smocks
red, yellow, orange, green, pink, and brown paint
large white paper

VOCABULARY

change	fall	growth	leaf	season
spring	summer	tree	winter	

WHAT TO DO

1. Talk with the children about how the seasons change and how with each passing season they can see how nature changes form. Explain to the children how they too grow with the year!
2. Have the children roll up their sleeves and put on smocks.
3. Paint each child's forearm from the elbow to the fingertips with brown paint and stamp it four times on a sheet of paper. These painted arms will be the tree trunks. (Alternatively, have the children put their arms down on the sheets of paper and paint four loose outlines each around their forearms and open hands.)
4. Wash the children's arms carefully.
5. After the children's arms are clean, set out the other colors of fingerpaint and invite the children to dip their fingertips into the paint and start decorating their four different trees, making one for each season.
6. Talk with the children as they work, asking them about their different trees and about the way they are painting their trees.
7. Let the paintings dry. Help the children sign their names next to their four trees, and then hang them in seasonal groups on the walls.

ASSESSMENT

To assess the children's learning, consider the following:
● Can the children describe the differences in a tree through the various seasons?
● Are the children able to decorate their trees according to the seasons?

Hilary Romig, Las Cruces, NM

Children's Books

Curious George: Seasons by H. A. Rey and Margaret Rey
Sunshine by Jan Ormerod
Sunshine Makes the Seasons by Franklyn M. Branley and Michael Rex

I'm Summer (Winter, Spring, or Fall)

Materials

- paper plates (4 per child)
- crayons, markers, or other art supplies
- hole punch (adult use only)
- string or yarn

LEARNING OBJECTIVES

The children will:
1. Learn about the seasons.
2. Learn how to anticipate which season comes next.
3. Develop their small motor skills.

VOCABULARY

fall   season   spring   summer   winter

WHAT TO DO

1. Gather the children together and talk about the seasons. Ask the children which seasons they prefer. Consider reading the children a book about the seasons.
2. Show the children the materials. Explain that they will be making masks for every season.
3. Invite the children to make their masks by drawing symbols of the seasons on them. Make suggestions, such as the sun for summer, a snowflake or snowman for the winter, and so on. Have season-related stickers the children can use if they have trouble drawing.
4. When the children finish decorating their masks, punch holes in the sides of the masks and attach string to them so the children can wear them.
5. Separate the children into small groups and have them guess which masks correspond to which seasons.

TEACHER-TO-TEACHER TIP

- Consider making a game with the masks, in which a child calls out a descriptive term that relates to a season, and the rest of the children put on their corresponding seasonal masks.

ASSESSMENT

To assess the children's learning, consider the following:
- Do the children understand the concept of four different seasons?
- What kinds of seasonal images do the children put on their masks?

Donna Alice Patton, Hillsboro, OH

Children's Books

Every Season by Shelley Rotner and Anne Love Woodhull
The Reasons for Seasons by Gail Gibbons
Season to Season by Jason Cooper

Butterfly Time

4+

LEARNING OBJECTIVES

The children will:
1. Learn about butterflies.
2. Develop their small motor skills.

butterfly stencil
construction paper
   in various colors
brown, orange,
   white, and black
   paint
paintbrushes
markers, crayons,
   and colored
   pencils
glitter
glue sticks
string
hole punch (adult
   use only)

VOCABULARY

butterfly   caterpillar   flower   fly   nectar

PREPARATION

● Use the butterfly stencil to make several construction-paper butterfly cutouts.

WHAT TO DO

1. Show the children several images of butterflies, and talk about the butterflies. Ask the children if they have ever seen butterflies outside. Ask the children what the butterflies were doing, and what they looked like. Talk about how butterflies only come out in late spring and summer because butterflies live off the nectar in blooming flowers and need warm weather to survive.

2. Set out the butterfly cutouts along with the other art materials and invite the children to decorate their butterflies.

3. When the children finish decorating their butterflies, help them write their names along the bottoms of the cutouts.

4. Punch holes in the tops of the butterflies and help the children tie thread to the butterflies. Hang the butterflies from the ceiling in various places around the room.

ASSESSMENT

To assess the children's learning, consider the following:
● Do the children understand why they see butterflies only in the warm weather?
● Are the children able to decorate their butterfly cutouts?

Children's Books

My, Oh My—A Butterfly by Tish Rabe
Nature's Children: Monarch Butterfly by Bill Ivy
The Very Hungry Caterpillar by Eric Carle

Ingelore Mix, Amherst, NH

Cotton Bud Snowflake

4+

LEARNING OBJECTIVES

The children will:
1. Learn that snowflakes have six points.
2. Develop their small motor skills.

Materials

images of snowflakes

waxed paper circles or squares

clear tape

cotton bud sticks or craft sticks

white glue in a squeeze bottle

glitter (other sparkly sprinkles, optional)

VOCABULARY

cold   season   shape   snow   snowflake   winter

WHAT TO DO

1. During the winter season, talk with the children about snow and snowflakes. Explain how snow is made up of many little individual snowflakes.
2. Read the children a book about snow and snowflakes (see the list to the left).
3. Show the children some images of snowflakes, and explain that the children will be making their own snowflakes.
4. Place waxed paper circles or squares on the work space. Tape the edges down to help keep the waxed paper from wrinkling.
5. In the center of each child's waxed paper, squeeze a puddle of white glue.
6. Invite the children to arrange cotton buds in the shapes of snowflakes and to use sticks to move the glue into interesting designs. Encourage the children to make snowflakes with six points, but allow them to make any shape.
7. Add a loop of ribbon or string before the glue dries in order to be able to hang the snowflake later.
8. Provide glitter that the children can sprinkle over their snowflake patterns.
9. Let the snowflakes dry for a day or two, or until the glue is clear.
10. Help the children peel their snowflakes carefully from the waxed paper. Hang the snowflakes from the ceiling around the room.

ASSESSMENT

To assess the children's learning, consider the following:
- Are the children able to make snowflakes?
- How many points do the children's snowflakes have?

MaryAnn F. Kohl, Bellingham, WA

Children's Books

Snow by Uri Shulevitz
Snowballs by Lois Ehlert
The Snowflake by Neil Waldman
Snowmen at Night by Caralyn Buehner
The Tiny Snowflake by Arthur Ginolfi

Fall Leaf Prints

4+

LEARNING OBJECTIVES

The children will:

1. Learn about the fall season.
2. Develop their small motor skills.

Materials

fallen leaves
plaster of Paris
bowl lids
paints and
  paintbrushes

VOCABULARY

autumn   fall   leaf   print   season   weather

WHAT TO DO

1. Engage the children in a discussion about the fall season. Ask the children to describe the season.
2. Lead the conversation to how, in the fall, leaves change colors and then fall from the trees.
3. Show the children the gathered fallen leaves and explain that the children will be making leaf prints.
4. Pour the plaster of Paris into individual bowl lids and give each child a leaf. (Alternatively, consider having the children go outside and choose their own fallen leaves to use for this activity.)
5. Show the children how to press their leaves into the plaster of Paris and then gently lift the leaves out and toss them in the trash.
6. When the children's molds harden, set out paints and brushes and invite the children to paint the molds in fall colors.

TEACHER-TO-TEACHER TIP

- Consider poking holes in the molds before they dry. The children can then tie strings through the molds and wear or hang their leaf creations.

ASSESSMENT

To assess the children's learning, consider the following:

- Do the children understand that leaves fall in the fall season?
- What colors are the children painting their leaf prints?

Children's Books

Autumn by Gerda Muller
I Know It's Autumn by Eileen Spinelli
The Pumpkin People by David Cavagnaro
The Tale of Squirrel Nutkin by Beatrix Potter

Cookie Zingarelli, Columbus, OH

Flowers Bloom in Spring

LEARNING OBJECTIVES

The children will:
1. Develop their observation skills.
2. Develop a respect for the environment.
3. Learn about nature in springtime.
4. Develop their small motor skills.

Materials

soft modeling clay
  in various colors
fresh flower petals
rolling pins

VOCABULARY

bud	earth	environment	flower bed	flower
grow	season	spring	sprout	

PREPARATION

- Set the materials on the children's work tables.
- Pick flower petals beforehand.
- Ask the children's families to bring in rolling pins for this activity.

WHAT TO DO

1. Read the children a book about springtime (see the list to the left for suggestions).
2. Talk with the children about how plants begin to bud in the springtime. Show the children the picked flower petals. Ask the children to talk about some of the flowers they have seen recently. Talk with the children about how spring weather is conducive to plants flowering.
3. At the work tables, give each child a small amount of modeling clay, letting each child choose the color.
4. Show the children how to press a flower petal into the clay, and then carefully pull the flower petal from the clay, leaving an impression. Help the children press various flower petals, making designs in the clay in the shapes of flower blossoms.

ASSESSMENT

To assess the children's learning, consider the following:
- Can the children tell you about their flowers?
- Do the children know why most flowers bloom in spring?
- Can the children tell you some of the different colors of flowers?

Shirley Anne Ramaley, Sun City, AZ

Children's Books

April Flowers by Donna Jo Napoli, Doron Ben-Ami, and Lauren Klementz-Harte
Colorful Spring by Erin Moran and Danny Pickett
Fletcher and the Springtime Blossoms by Julia Rawlinson and Tiphanie Beeke
Why Do Plants Grow in Spring? by Helen Orme

Painting Spring Trees

4+

LEARNING OBJECTIVES

The children will:

1. Create pictures of trees with paper and paint.
2. Familiarize themselves with the color green.
3. Develop their small motor skills.

Materials

brown and white
  construction
  paper
glue
sponges
paint trays
green tempera
  paint

VOCABULARY

brown   green   leaf   spring   tree   trunk   white

PREPARATION

- Moisten the sponge pieces and fill the paint trays with green tempera paint.

WHAT TO DO

1. Explain to the children that many trees grow new leaves in the spring. Tell them that they are going to create pictures of spring trees.
2. Have each child tear a tree trunk out of brown paper and glue it on a sheet of white paper.
3. Ask the children to dip the sponge pieces in the green paint and use them to paint leaves on their tree trunks.
4. When the paintings are dry, hang them up in the classroom for the children to look at and discuss.

SONG

The Buds on the Trees by Laura Wynkoop
(Tune: "The Wheels on the Bus")

The buds on the trees are opening up,
Opening up, opening up.
The buds on the trees are opening up,
All through the town.

The leaves on the trees are soft and green,
Soft and green, soft and green.
The leaves on the trees are soft and green,
All through the town.

The branches on the trees dance in
* the breeze,*
In the breeze, in the breeze.
The branches on the trees dance in
* the breeze,*
All through the town.

Children's Books

Franklin Plants a Tree
  by Sharon Jennings
A Tree for Me by Nancy
  Van Laan
A Tree Is Nice by Janice
  May Udry

ASSESSMENT

To assess the children's learning, consider the following:

- Can the children identify the color they used in their paintings?
- Are the children able to paint pictures of trees?

Laura Wynkoop, San Dimas, CA

Snow People

LEARNING OBJECTIVES

The children will:
1. Learn to work together.
2. Develop their large motor skills.

Materials

large piece of butcher paper
black construction paper
scissors (adult use only)
glue sticks

VOCABULARY

build	button	circle	eye	face
large	medium	mouth	nose	scarf
small	snow	winter		

PREPARATION

● Cut three circles of varying size out of butcher paper (one set per pair of children).
● Cut several small black circles to serve as facial features and buttons.
● Consider making a model from which the children can work.

WHAT TO DO

1. Ask the children if they have ever built snow people before. Talk with the children about what they need to do so.
2. Tell the children they will be building snow people inside today.
3. Show the children the paper cutouts and glue.
4. Separate the children into pairs. Give each pair a set of white circles in varying sizes, as well as several smaller black circles.
5. Invite each pair of children to work together to build their snow person. Talk about the order of the white circles, asking which is largest and smallest. Allow the children to put the circles together in any way they like.
6. When the children have built their snow people, hang them together on the wall.

TEACHER-TO-TEACHER TIPS

● Use paint smocks. This activity is messy, but worth it.
● Consider providing real twigs for arms.

Children's Books

The Snowman by Raymond Briggs
The Snowy Day by Ezra Jack Keats
Winter by Gerda Muller

ASSESSMENT

To assess the children's learning, consider the following:
● Do the children understand which season is best for making snow people?
● How well do the children work with their partners when making their snow people?

Carla LeMasters, Bartonville, IL

Tree Seasons

4+

LEARNING OBJECTIVES

The children will:
1. Develop their small motor skills.
2. Learn the names of the four seasons.
3. Learn about how the seasons affect trees.

Materials

paper (4 sheets per child)
cotton swabs
tree shape cutout
marker
white, light green, orange, red, brown, and yellow paint
½" strips of green tissue paper
Q-tips
½" paintbrushes
glue

VOCABULARY

bloom	branch	fall	leaf	spring
summer	tree	trunk	winter	

PREPARATION

● Use the tree shape cutout to draw basic tree outlines on all the sheets of paper.

WHAT TO DO

1. Gather the children together and read a book about trees through the seasons (see list to the left).
2. Talk with the children about what happens to trees through the seasons, including how the trees change shape and color.
3. Set out the paper and other materials. Invite the children to paint and decorate one image of a tree in each season. Talk with the children about their pictures as they work, guiding them toward season-appropriate imagery. **Note:** The children can use the strips of green tissue paper to make leaves to glue to the trees for the summer season.

TEACHER-TO-TEACHER TIP

● Consider posting the children's pictures together by name or by season and challenging the children to find their own images and say which seasons they represent.

ASSESSMENT

To assess the children's learning, consider the following:
● Can the children describe how the various seasons affect trees?
● Are the children able to make tree paintings for each separate season?

Children's Books

Four Seasons Make a Year by Anne Rockwell and Megan Halsey
Tree for All Seasons by Robin Bernard
Watching the Seasons by Edana Eckart

Sandie Nagel, White Lake, MI

Seasonal Placemats

5+

LEARNING OBJECTIVES

The children will:
1. Learn about the four seasons.
2. Create a practical object.
3. Develop their small motor skills.

Materials

sheet of 8" x 10" poster board per child (white is best for drawing, colored is better for adding on pictures)

clear contact paper (enough to cover poster board front and back)

crayons, markers, and pencils

ruler

seasonal images cut from magazines

VOCABULARY

fall   season   spring   summer   winter

WHAT TO DO

1. Give each child a piece of poster board.
2. Divide each side of poster board into two equal parts by drawing a line down the middle of each side (two seasons per side).
3. Help the children write the names of the seasons at the tops of the squares.
4. Try to group summer/spring and winter/fall together.
5. Set out markers, pencils, and crayons, and invite the children to draw season-appropriate images in each season's box. Also make precut images available for the children to glue into the boxes.
6. After the children finish decorating the sections of their poster board, help the children sign their boards and then laminate them for durability.
7. Invite the children to use their placemats for snack time.

TEACHER-TO-TEACHER TIPS

- This makes a great activity for Family Night. Parents, family members, and children can take the placemats home to reinforce the concept of seasons.
- Ask the children to bring seasonal pictures cut from magazines from home; or provide time for the children to cut out the pictures in class.

ASSESSMENT

To assess the children's learning, consider the following:
- Do the children know that each season has specific symbols—snow in the winter, flowers in the spring, leaves falling in the fall?
- Can the children place appropriate pictures under each season?

Donna Alice Patton, Hillsboro, OH

Children's Books

Four Seasons Make a Year by Anne Rockwell and Megan Halsey
Seasons by Jim Pipe
The Seasons of the Year: Everything Science by Marcia S. Freeman
Sunshine Makes the Seasons by Franklyn M. Branley

Hello, Spring

3+

LEARNING OBJECTIVES

The children will:

1. Listen and follow a story.
2. Participate in a group activity.
3. Recall and describe the details of a story.

Materials

The Happy Day by Ruth Krauss and Marc Simont large photographs of each animal in the book

VOCABULARY

bear   field mouse   groundhog   season   snail   spring   squirrel

WHAT TO DO

1. Organize the children in groups to represent each animal in *The Happy Day* by Ruth Krauss and Marc Simont.
2. Give each group of children one large image of one of the animals in the story. Explain to those children that they will pay specific close attention to what that animal does in the story.

3. Read *The Happy Day* aloud to the children. While reading the story, invite each group of "animals" to act out the actions of the animals in the story. For example, the children can act out sleeping, waking up, sniffing, running (by sitting on the floor and tapping their feet as if running), dancing, and so on.
4. After finishing the story, talk with the children about what all the creatures did on that fine spring day. Challenge the children to recall what all the animals did.

TEACHER-TO-TEACHER TIP

- Read the story once before having children participate, and then read the story again, having the children participate in the reading. Practice the actions together before playing parts.

ASSESSMENT

To assess the children's learning, consider the following:

- Are the children able to make motions that mimic those of the animals in the book?
- Do the children listen and make the motions for their animal groups at the right times?

Children's Books

It's Spring by Linda Glaser
Spring by Núria Roca
Spring Things by Bob Raczka

Sandra Ryan, Buffalo, NY

Name That Season!

3+

LEARNING OBJECTIVES

The children will:
1. Guess the answer to a riddle.
2. Name the seasons of the year.

Materials

VOCABULARY

fall   season   spring   summer   weather   winter

WHAT TO DO

1. Read *Four Seasons Make a Year* by Anne Rockwell with the children. Discuss the four seasons and things people do in each one.
2. Recite the following riddles to the children, challenging them to guess which season each riddle refers to:

Riddles by Susan Oldham Hill
(Tune: "Mary Had a Little Lamb")
Snow is falling all around, on the ground, all around.
I'm a season very cold. Can you guess my name?

Flowers are blooming everywhere, and right there, everywhere.
I'm a season that's fresh and cool. Can you guess my name?

Friends go swimming at the beach, at the beach, at the beach.
I'm a season that gets so hot. Can you guess my name?

Now the air is crisp and cool, crisp and cool, crisp and cool.
I'm a season of giving thanks. Can you guess my name?

Christmastime will soon be here, such good cheer! soon be here.
I'm a season of giving gifts. Can you guess my name?

Baby animals will be born, in the morn, will be born.
I'm a season of brand new life. Can you guess my name?

Let's go to the pumpkin patch, pumpkin patch, pumpkin patch.
This is harvest time for sure. Can you guess my name?

All the leaves are dark and green, dark and green, dark and green.
The sun is shining down on me. Can you guess my name?

ASSESSMENT

To assess the children's learning, consider the following:
- Can the children solve the riddles?
- Can the children name the seasons?

Susan Oldham Hill, Lakeland, FL

Children's Books

Four Seasons Make a Year by Anne Rockwell
Sunshine Makes the Seasons by Franklyn M. Branley
A Tree for All Seasons by Robin Bernard

Parade of Seasons

3+

The children will:
1. Learn the names of the seasons.
2. Develop their small motor skills.
3. Learn the words of a song.

Materials

construction paper for headbands
stapler (adult use only)
2" cutouts of suns, snowflakes, fall leaves, and flowers
glue
markers

VOCABULARY

fall   season   spring   summer   weather   winter

WHAT TO DO

1. Read *The Reasons for Seasons* by Gail Gibbons and discuss the four seasons with the children.
2. Ask the children to choose their favorite season. Show the children how to pick the cutouts that match the season they chose: summer = sun; winter = snowflake; fall = leaves; spring = flowers.
3. Give the children markers to decorate the cutouts and the headbands, and demonstrate how to glue the cutout on the center of the headbands.
4. Teacher-only step: Staple the headbands so they fit the children comfortably.
5. Teach the children the following song:

   Seasons Marching by Susan Oldham Hill
   (Tune: "Camptown Races")
   Seasons marching all around:
   Summer, winter!
   Seasons marching up and down:
   Spring and fall, hooray!
   Summertime is hot;
   Spring flowers all around.
   Winter snowflakes in the air,
   And fall sees leaves come down.

6. Invite the children to march around, wearing their headbands and singing the song. Add rhythm instruments for extra fun.

ASSESSMENT

To assess the children's learning, consider the following:
- Can the children name the seasons of the year?
- Are the children able to make colorful headbands?
- Can the children learn the words to "Seasons Marching"?

Children's Books

The Reasons for Seasons by Gail Gibbons
Sunshine Makes the Seasons by Franklyn M. Branley
Watching the Seasons by Edana Eckart

Susan Oldham Hill, Lakeland, FL

Pile of Leaves

3+

LEARNING OBJECTIVES

The children will:
1. Use small motor skills to make a self-portrait.
2. Learn to trace handprints.
3. Learn about the fall season.

Materials

Why Do Leaves Change Color? by Betsy Maestro
crayons and markers
mirrors
scissors (adult use only)
glue
2" leaf cutouts (or tissue squares)
9" x 12" construction paper

VOCABULARY

autumn   fall   leaf   season   weather

WHAT TO DO

1. Read *Why Do Leaves Change Color?* by Betsy Maestro several times with the children, discussing the process of color change.
2. Show the children the piles of leaves on pages 24, 25, 28, and 29 of the book. Ask the children whether they have played in leaf piles before. Put the book in the book area for the children to read independently.
3. Give each child markers, crayons, and a sheet of construction paper. Ask the children to draw their faces only. Encourage the children to look in mirrors to have a clear sense of what they look like.
4. Give each child a second sheet of paper for hand tracing. Ask the children to work in pairs, helping each other trace their hands.
5. Outline the faces with a marker and help the children cut the faces out. Fold the pages with the traced handprints and cut out two copies of each hand.
6. Give each child paper and assorted leaf cutouts or tissue squares. Show the children the picture on page 28 of *Why Do Leaves Change Color?*, explaining that the children are making a leaf pile similar to the one on that page.
7. When the leaves are all piled up and glued on, the children then glue their faces and hands on top of the leaves, so it will look like they are covered with leaves and only their heads and hands show, just like the picture on page 28 of the book.
8. Help the children glue the face and hand cutouts on top of their leaves.

ASSESSMENT

To assess the children's learning, consider the following:
- Can the children use small motor skills to color and trace?
- Can the children identify the season in which leaves fall from the trees?

Susan Oldham Hill, Lakeland, FL

Children's Books

Red Leaf, Yellow Leaf by Lois Ehlert
Sunshine Makes the Seasons by Franklyn M. Branley
Watching the Seasons by Edana Eckart

Snowflakes Are Different, and So Are You

3+

Materials

The Snowflake by
Neil Waldman
(or similar book)
images of
snowflakes

LEARNING OBJECTIVES

The children will:
1. Learn why snowflakes all look different.
2. Recognize each child is also different and special.
3. Develop their large motor skills.

VOCABULARY

design   season   snow   snowflake   weather   winter

WHAT TO DO

1. Read Neil Waldman's *The Snowflake* to the children. Talk with the children about how snowflakes are made, and how each snowflake is different. Explain that as the water droplets fall through the air, bits of dust stick to them. The water droplets then freeze into snowflakes, making beautiful designs.
2. Show the children photographs of snowflakes and invite the children to compare the images. Pay special attention to how each snowflake is unique.
3. Challenge the children to think of how each child in the classroom is unique and special. Note some differences and let the children add their own observations, such as how one child has dimples and curly hair, another child knows about dinosaurs, another child is tall or can tell stories, and so on.
4. Teach the children the following fingerplay:

Snowflakes Are Different, and So Are You by Kay Flowers
Snowflakes falling through the air, (flutter fingers in downward motion)
Snowflakes landing in my hair, (look surprised and pleased)
Just like this! (tap head with fingertips three times to accent each word)

Watching snowflakes as they fall; (chin in hands as if deep in thought)
They don't look the same at all, (shrug and hold out hands, palms up)
Just like YOU! (point to three separate children to accent each word)

ASSESSMENT

To assess the children's learning, consider the following:
- Do the children note and appreciate individual differences among themselves?
- Can the children point to differences and similarities between images of snowflakes?

Children's Books

Ken Libbrecht's Field Guide to Snowflakes by Ken Libbrecht
Snowflake Bentley by Jacqueline Briggs Martin
The Tiny Snowflake Picture Book by Arthur Ginolfi

Kay Flowers, Summerfield, OH

The Snowman

3+

LEARNING OBJECTIVES

The children will:
1. Learn about winter weather.
2. Learn about snowmen.
3. Develop their listening skills.

Materials

The Snowman by
Raymond Briggs
plush toy snowman

VOCABULARY

body	carrot	cold	head	hot	medium
middle	nose	small	snowball	snowman	

PREPARATION
● Hide the plush toy snowman somewhere in the room.

WHAT TO DO
1. Gather a few children together and talk to them about the winter season. Ask the children if they have ever made or seen a snowman.
2. Read Raymond Briggs's *The Snowman* to the children. Discuss the story with the children. Challenge them to recall and describe the story.
3. Tell the children there is a toy snowman hidden somewhere in the classroom for them to find.
4. Invite the children to look through the classroom for the snowman. Use the words "hot" and "cold" to let the children know how close to or far from finding the snowman they are.
5. After the children find the snowman, consider hiding the snowman again and repeating the activity, if the children show interest.

TEACHER-TO-TEACHER TIP
● Consider having the child who finds the snowman hide it for the next round, and having this child direct the other children by saying "hot" and "cold" as they search for the snowman.

Children's Books

Sadie and the Snowman by Allen Morgan
Snowballs by Lois Ehlert
The Snowman by Raymond Briggs

ASSESSMENT
To assess the children's learning, consider the following:
● Can the children describe the story of *The Snowman?*
● Do the children pay attention to the "hot" and "cold" clues to adjust their search for the snowman?

Jackie Wright, Enid, OK

Clouds in Every Season

4+

LEARNING OBJECTIVES

The children will:
1. Learn about clouds.
2. Develop their small motor skills.

Materials

poster board
markers
cotton
glue

VOCABULARY

cloud   season   summer   weather   wind   winter

PREPARATION

- Cut four large cloud shapes out of paper or poster board.
- Write the name of a different season on each cloud cutout.

WHAT TO DO

1. Read the children a book about clouds (see suggestions to the left).
2. Talk with the children about how there are clouds in every season. Ask the children to describe the clouds from different seasons. Do clouds in the summertime make snow?
3. Show the children the large cloud cutouts.
4. Provide the children with cotton balls and glue. Invite the children to glue their cotton balls to the various clouds.
5. Ask the children to pick the current season's cloud and then hang it from the ceiling. Change the cloud as the seasons pass.

Children's Books

Hi, Clouds by Carol Greene
It Looked Like Spilt Milk by Charles Green Shaw
Little Cloud by Eric Carle
Mushroom in the Rain by Mirra Ginsburg
Stormy Weather by Debi Gliori
Today's Weather Is by Lorraine Jean Hopping

ASSESSMENT

To assess the children's learning, consider the following:
- Can the children identify the current season?
- Do the children understand that clouds are common in every season?

Cookie Zingarelli, Columbus, OH

Leaf People

4+

LEARNING OBJECTIVES

The children will:
1. Learn about how leaves fall in the autumn.
2. Develop their small motor skills.
3. Make leaf people or leaf animals.

Materials

Leaf Man by Lois Ehlert
real leaves or pictures of different kinds of leaves
construction paper
glue sticks
googly eyes

VOCABULARY

autumn   fall   leaf   person   season

WHAT TO DO

1. Gather the children together and read them Lois Ehlert's *Leaf Man*.
2. Discuss leaves with the children, focusing on how leaves fall in the autumn.
3. Bring the children outside and have them collect leaves. Return to the classroom with the children.
4. Provide construction paper, glue sticks, markers, and googly eyes the children can use to make leaf people and leaf animals from the leaves they find. Help the children glue their leaf people and animals to the construction paper. The children may draw directly on the leaves, as well as on the paper around the leaves.
5. Talk with the children about their leaf creations. Ask the children what their leaf creations' names are, and so on.
6. Hang the leaf people and leaf animals in the classroom.

SONG

Leaf Man by Kristen Peters
(Tune: "Are You Sleeping")
Where is leaf man? Where is leaf man?
Made of leaves, made of leaves.
Yellow, red, and orange;
Green, brown, and purple;
Colors are seen, colors are seen.

ASSESSMENT

To assess the children's learning, consider the following:
- Can the children identify the season in which leaves fall?
- What kind of leaf people and leaf animals do the children create?

Kristen Peters, Mattituck, NY

Children's Books

The Leaves Fall All Around by Steve Mack
Leaves, Leaves by Salina Yoon
Red Leaf, Yellow Leaf by Lois Ehlert
Why Do Leaves Change Color? by Betsy Maestro

Maple Leaf Stenciling

4+

LEARNING OBJECTIVES

The children will:
1. Recognize the shape of a maple leaf.
2. Use small motor skills to stencil.

Materials

Red Leaf, Yellow Leaf by Lois Ehlert
acetate sheets or heavy cardboard
scissors (adult use only)
red and yellow paint
shallow containers
sponges or stencil brushes
masking tape
10" x 12" pieces of burlap or another knobby weave fabric (paper also works)

PREPARATION

- Trace maple leaf shapes on five sheets of acetate or heavy cardboard.
- Cut out the shapes.

WHAT TO DO

1. Read the children Lois Ehlert's *Red Leaf, Yellow Leaf* and discuss the maple leaf shape. Point out the stencil on the first page and the one on the last page of the story.
2. Discuss the red and yellow leaves on that last page and explain about leaves changing color (information on the last pages of the book).
3. Give each child a piece of fabric. Show the children how to place the stencil on the fabric and tape it in place. Show the children how to dab the sponge gently into the paint, wipe off the excess, and dab or pounce the sponge on the stencil. Make sure the children dab on the edges to reveal the border of the leaf.
4. Encourage the children to reposition the stencil and paint a leaf in a new shape. Remind the children to stencil at least one leaf with red and one with yellow paint. If the paint blends as the children move the stencils, it will look even more realistic.
5. Hang the stenciled banners in the classroom.

ASSESSMENT

To assess the children's learning, consider the following:
- Can the children recognize the maple leaf in a group of other leaf shapes?
- Are the children able to use a stencil effectively to make the leaf banner?

Susan Oldham Hill, Lakeland, FL

Children's Books

Leaves by David Ezra Stein
Sunshine Makes the Seasons by Franklyn M. Branley
Watching the Seasons by Edana Eckart

Planting Sprouted Seeds

4+

LEARNING OBJECTIVES

The children will:
1. Learn how to sprout seeds.
2. Learn how to plant sprouted seeds.

Materials

Watch It Grow, Watch It Change by Joan Elma Rahn (or similar book)

large seeds (such as squash or melon)

sturdy white paper towels

clear plastic zipper-lock bags

potting soil

paper cups (or encourage recycling by planting in clean, used, individual-serving yogurt cups)

plastic squeeze condiment bottle

Children's Books

From Seed to Plant by Gail Gibbons
Seeds Sprout! by Mary Dodson Wade
The Tiny Seed by Eric Carle

VOCABULARY

grow   harvest   season   seed   spring   sprout   summer

PREPARATION

- Fill the plastic condiment bottle with clear water.
- Write each child's name on a plastic bag.

WHAT TO DO

1. Read Joan Elma Rahn's *Watch It Grow, Watch It Change* to the children.
2. Talk with the children about the season when people plant and grow things. Ask the children if they have ever seen or helped people plant seeds.
3. Explain to the children that seeds usually sprout in the ground but that they are going to see seeds sprouting before they get planted.
4. Show the children how to dribble water gently on a paper towel, place two seeds on the paper towel, fold it over the seeds, and place it in their plastic bag.
5. Stack the plastic bags in a dark, warm place. Let the children check for sprouts every day, dribbling more water on the paper towels if they are not moist.
6. When tiny sprouts appear, poke three holes in the bottom of a cup, add the potting soil, and plant the seeds, sprout side up. Moisten with water and place in sunny spot.

TEACHER-TO-TEACHER TIP

- Plant some unsprouted seeds at the same time the sprouted seeds are planted and then observe which ones pop through the soil first.

ASSESSMENT

To assess the children's learning, consider the following:
- Do the children show interest in the appearance of the sprouts?
- Can the children plant and water their seeds with a minimum of help?

Kay Flowers, Summerfield, OH

Winter Summer Listening Activity

4+

Materials

book about seasons
plastic drinking
    straws
yellow paper sun
    shapes
yellow curling
    ribbon cut into
    8" strands
transparent tape
white tissue paper

LEARNING OBJECTIVES

The children will:
1. Improve their understanding of the seasons.
2. Develop their listening skills.
3. Learn to follow directions.

VOCABULARY

season   snow   snowball   summer   sun   winter

PREPARATION

- Create a sunshine wand for each child: Tape three strands of yellow curling ribbon and a yellow paper sun shape to the one end of a straw.

WHAT TO DO

1. Provide each child with a piece of white tissue paper. Have the children crumple these into balls to create the snowballs for this activity.
2. Give each child a sunshine wand. Read the children a book about the seasons (see list to the left for suggestions). Invite the children to hold up their snowballs whenever they hear about winter weather and to wave their sunshine wands over their heads whenever they hear about warm summer weather.
3. After reading the book, recite simple statements about winter and summer such as "I went sledding down the hill at my grandpa's farm," "Our family went swimming at the lake," "We like to make a snow fort in our yard," and "Dad cooked hamburgers on the grill outside."
4. Challenge the children to raise the correct object during each statement.
5. Encourage the children to work in groups in which the children take turns stating a favorite summertime or wintertime activity, and the rest of the children wave their sunshine wands or snowballs accordingly.

ASSESSMENT

To assess the children's learning, consider the following:
- Do the children understand the connection between the objects and the seasons?
- Are the children attentive? Do they wave the correct objects during the various seasonal statements?
- Can the children describe things they like about the two seasons?

Children's Books

Seasons and Weather
    by David Evans
The Sun Is So Quiet by
    Nikki Giovanni
Sunshine by Gail
    Saunders-Smith

Mary J. Murray, Mazomanie, WI

Leaves Are Falling Down   3+

LEARNING OBJECTIVES

The children will:
1. Learn about how leaves fall in autumn.
2. Learn the names of autumn colors.

Materials

real fallen leaves

VOCABULARY

autumn   brown   fall   orange   season   yellow

PREPARATION

● Prior to this activity, go outside with the children and have each child choose a fallen leaf to bring inside. Alternatively, consider bringing in store-bought artificial leaves.

WHAT TO DO

1. Gather the children together and talk with them about their fallen leaves. Ask the children to identify the leaves' colors, and to talk about how the leaves feel.
2. Teach the children the following action rhyme:

The Wind Is Blowing by Ingelore Mix
The wind is blowing, blowing, (children weave back and forth)
And leaves are falling down.
First fall all the yellows, (children with yellow leaves sit down)
Then red, (children holding red leaves sit down)
And orange, (children holding orange leaves sit down)
And now brown. (children holding brown leaves sit down)

3. After the children complete the rhyme, invite them to trade leaves with the other children and recite the rhyme again.

ASSESSMENT

To assess the children's learning, consider the following:
● Can the children say what leaves do in the fall?
● Can the children name the colors leaves turn in the fall? Can the children identify these colors on their leaves?

Ingelore Mix, Amherst, NH

Children's Books

Autumn by Steven Schnur
It's Fall! by Linda Glaser
Now It's Fall by Lois Lenski
Ten Apples Up On Top by Dr. Seuss

The Season Symbol Sort

3+

LEARNING OBJECTIVES

The children will:
1. Group objects based on season.
2. Learn about how symbols function.

Materials

boxes with 3–4
   seasonal objects
   (1 box per
   season)
cardboard sun
cardboard
   snowflake
cardboard fall tree
cardboard flower
   bud

VOCABULARY

autumn	fall	season	sort
spring	summer	symbol	winter

WHAT TO DO

1. Ask the children which season they like the best. Ask the children to talk about their choices.
2. Show the children a seasonal object (such as a mitten or a sand pail) and ask them what the object is and which season they associate the object with.

3. Set the items in the properly labeled box.
4. Explain to the children that making these groups is called sorting.
5. After the children sort all the objects into the correct boxes, show the children the four different cardboard images.
6. Challenge the children to indicate which season each image represents. Explain that these images are symbols, and talk with the children about what symbols are. Ask the children if they have seen other symbols before. Give examples, such as elevator and bathroom signs.

ASSESSMENT

To assess the children's learning, consider the following:
- Can the children sort the objects correctly?
- Do the children understand the principle of sorting?
- Do the children understand what symbols are?

Debbie Vilardi, Commack, NY

Children's Books

Babar's Busy Year by Laurent de Brunhoff
Listen, Listen! by Phillis Gershator
Watching the Seasons by Edana Eckart

Summer Flowers

3+

LEARNING OBJECTIVES

The children will:
1. Learn to identify colors by name.
2. Learn about various flowers.
3. Learn to cooperate and follow directions.

Materials

colored tissue
  paper
scissors (adult use
  only)
bread twist-ties
flower wand (a
  paper flower
  taped to an
  unsharpened
  pencil with
  strands of
  colorful curling
  ribbon attached)

VOCABULARY

circle	color	flower	grow	listen
pick	sit	walk	wand	

PREPARATION

● Make one colorful tissue paper flower per child by cutting sheets of tissue paper into circles and squares, setting three sheets on top of each other, holding them at the center, and twisting them into shape.

WHAT TO DO

1. Invite the children to stand in a circle and join hands.
2. Display the assorted flowers in the center of the circle, scattered randomly.
3. Hand the flower wand to one child and have the child stand in the center of the circle to become the "flower fairy."
4. Ask the children to walk around the circle of flowers, in a counterclockwise direction, as they recite the following chant in unison:

   Walk around the flowers
   Growing on the ground.
   Pretty summer flowers.
   All sit down!

5. As the chant ends, all the children sit down quickly.
6. The person in the middle then uses the wand to tap various classmates, signaling each one to pick a flower, say its color, and then carry it back to her place.
7. The activity continues until each of the children picks a flower.

ASSESSMENT

To assess the children's learning, consider the following:
● Are the children able to follow directions?
● Can the children recognize the colors of their flowers?

Mary J. Murray, Mazomanie, WI

Children's Books

Flower Garden by Eve
  Bunting
The Garden Party by
  James Hoffman
*A Kid's Guide to How
  Flowers Grow* by
  Patricia Ayers
Planting a Rainbow by
  Lois Ehlert

Let the Seasons Shine

4+

LEARNING OBJECTIVES

The children will:
1. Learn about the different seasons.
2. Begin to classify based on season.
3. Learn a poem about the seasons.

Materials

picture-word cards
for winter,
summer, spring,
and fall
5–10 pictures for
each season of
seasonal items
such as
snowflakes and
sleds, pumpkins
and leaves,
beach balls and
watermelons,
and flowers and
birds
bag or box for the
pictures of
seasonal items
flashlight

VOCABULARY

fall   season   spring   summer   temperature   weather   winter

WHAT TO DO

1. Discuss the seasons with the children, using the picture-word cards for winter, summer, spring, and fall.
2. Take a seasonal card from the bag and ask the children to identify the picture. Discuss when this item or activity would happen: spring, summer, winter, or fall.
3. Place the picture-word cards on the rug face-up and turn out the lights. Ask a child to shine the flashlight on the right season card. Then ask another child to put the seasonal picture under the correct heading.
4. Invite another child to draw a new card from the bag.
5. Ask her to name the picture and shine the flashlight on the correct heading.
6. Invite another child to place the picture in the correct category. If the card is placed in the wrong slot, discuss the choice with the children and help them see the correct placement.

POEM

The Seasons by Susan Oldham Hill
Winter, summer, spring and fall.
What's the best one of them all?
Summer heat and winter snow;
Leaves that fall and flowers that grow.
Winter, summer, spring and fall.
What's the best one of them all?

ASSESSMENT

To assess the children's learning, consider the following:
● Can the children differentiate between the seasons?
● Are the children able to match images to the correct seasons?
● Can the children recite the rhyme?

Children's Books

Frog and Toad All Year
by Arnold Lobel
The Reasons for Seasons
by Gail Gibbons
*Sunshine Makes the
Seasons* by Franklyn M.
Branley
Watching the Seasons
by Edana Eckart

Susan Oldham Hill, Lakeland, FL

My Life as a Plant

4+

LEARNING OBJECTIVES

The children will:

1. Learn about the life cycle of a plant.
2. Practice large motor skills.
3. Act out what they imagine life as a plant might be throughout the seasons.

Materials

VOCABULARY

bloom	dormant	fall	plant	seed
spring	summer	sway	winter	

WHAT TO DO

1. Talk with the children about plants. Ask the children if their families have plants growing in their homes.
2. Read the children one or more books about the life cycle of a plant (see list to the left).
3. After reading and discussing the book, have the children spread out so they have room to move.
4. Ask the children to imagine they are all seeds, lying dormant in the ground in winter. Have the children curl up in balls on the ground.
5. Now have the children imagine the rain is falling all around them in spring. Have them drum their hands on the ground to make the sound of the rain falling.
6. Ask the children to imagine the sun is coming out, warming them up. Have them rise up slowly like growing plants.
7. Tell the children to imagine it is summer, time for plants to start blooming. Invite the children to open up their arms like flowers blooming in the sun.
8. After a short while, tell the children it is becoming fall. Cold winds are starting to blow. Have the children make the noise of the cold wind, and have them sway like plants in the wind.
9. Tell the children it is now becoming winter, and the plant is becoming dormant. Have the children shrink back down into a ball on the ground.

Children's Books

From Seed to Plant by
Gail Gibbons
A Seed Is Sleepy by
Dianna Hutts Aston
The Tiny Seed by Eric
Carle

ASSESSMENT

To assess the children's learning, consider the following:

- Do the children participate in the activity?
- Can the children move their bodies as instructed?

Janet Hammond, Mount Laurel, NJ

A Sense of Seasons

4+

LEARNING OBJECTIVES

The children will:

1. Develop an awareness of events and activities associated with the change of seasons.
2. Participate in season-related group discussion.
3. Increase their knowledge of seasonal activities in other climates.

Materials

chart paper with columns labeled with season names and rows labeled with the five senses

season- and sense-related pictures

paper

crayons or markers

VOCABULARY

| fall | feel | hear | season | see | sense |
| smell | spring | summer | taste | touch | winter |

PREPARATION

● Prepare art area for activity.
● Display chart paper for children's responses.

WHAT TO DO

1. Gather the children together and engage them in a discussion about the seasons. Can the children name the current season? Can they name all the seasons and tell the order in which they occur?
2. Next, talk with the children about the five senses, asking them to name and describe the senses. Help the children if necessary.
3. Ask the children to name things that they see, hear, taste, smell, and feel in each season, focusing on one season at a time.
4. Have the children point out where on the chart their answers would belong.
5. Invite the children to draw pictures of the things they hear, see, feel, taste, or smell during their favorite seasons.

ASSESSMENT

To assess the children's learning, consider the following:

● Can the children associate a sensory experience or activity with a particular season?
● Can the children express appropriate ideas to add to the chart?

Margery Kranyik Fermino, West Roxbury, MA

Children's Books

Best Times Ever: A Book About Seasons and Holidays by Richard Scarry
My Five Senses by Aliki
You Can't Taste a Pickle with Your Ear by Harriet Ziefert and Amanda Haley

Dress a Snowperson

LEARNING OBJECTIVES

The children will:
1. Identify parts of the body.
2. Identify clothing.
3. Use one-to-one correspondence to count items.
4. Place clothing on the body appropriately.

Materials

3 boxes (large, medium, small)
roll of white bulletin board paper
large 6-sided die
clothing pieces for snowperson (scarf, hat, pants, and so on)

VOCABULARY

| boot | coat | frost | glove | jacket |
| mitten | scarf | snow | snowperson | temperature |

PREPARATION

● Wrap each box in white paper.
● Attach each box starting with the large one on the bottom, the medium-sized one in the middle, and the smallest one at the top.
● Provide numerous pieces of the snowperson's labeled clothing and label each feature and article of winter clothing.

WHAT TO DO

1. Talk with the children about snow and snowpersons. Ask the children if they have ever built or seen snowpersons.
2. Show the children the box snowperson. Spread out the articles of clothing, naming each one for the children and showing them where the names are on each item.
3. Ask the children to imagine how the snowperson feels in the snow with no clothes on. Tell the children they can help keep the snowperson warm by dressing it.
4. Invite the children to take turns rolling the die, and then counting the number of dots on the exposed face of the die. Then have the child add that number of articles of clothing to the snowperson, naming the items as she goes, as well as describing what part of the snowperson each item is covering.

ASSESSMENT

To assess the children's learning, consider the following:
● Can the children name the snowperson's body parts (neck, ears, legs, arms) they are covering with the clothes?
● Can the children count the number of dots on the die?

Children's Books

All You Need for a Snowman by Alice Schertle
Friendly Snowman by Sharon Gordon
The Jacket I Wear in the Snow by Shirley Neitzel
Our Snowman by M.B. Goffstein
The Snowman by Raymond Briggs
Snowmen at Night by Caralyn Buehner
Thomas' Snowsuit by Robert Munsch

Kaethe Lewandowski, Centreville, VA

Summer Cookout

4+

LEARNING OBJECTIVES

The children will:
1. Role-play cooking and serving food.
2. Improve their social skills.
3. Develop their motor skills.

Materials

felt or craft foam in the following colors: pink, peach, light brown, dark brown
small outdoor grill
spatula
tongs
paper plates and other picnic tableware
apron
empty mustard and ketchup bottles

VOCABULARY

bratwurst	charcoal	cook	grill	hamburger	hot
hot dog	onion	pepper	serve	spatula	tongs

PREPARATION

- Cut hot dog, bratwurst, hamburger, onion, pepper, and bun shapes from the felt or craft foam.
- Display all the materials in the dramatic play area of the classroom.

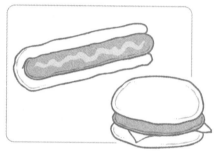

WHAT TO DO

1. Set the grill out in the dramatic play area and talk with the children about times they have eaten at barbecues. Ask the children what they ate at those barbecues, and what the weather was like.
2. Show the children the materials, and invite them to take turns pretending to cook and serve the "food."

TEACHER-TO-TEACHER TIP

- Consider asking a child's family member to lend a grill and grilling tools for the class to use for dramatic play.

ASSESSMENT

To assess the children's learning, consider the following:
- Do the children cooperate and work together to cook, serve, and "eat" the grilled sandwiches?
- Are children able to use the tools to manipulate the meat pieces on the grill?

Mary J. Murray, Mazomanie, WI

Children's Books

A Barbecue for Charlotte by Marc Tetro
Classroom Cookout by Susan Blackaby
Cookout at Grandma's House by Paulette Mack
Quite Enough Hot Dogs by Wil Mara

'Tis the Season

LEARNING OBJECTIVES

The children will:
1. Identify season-appropriate activities.
2. Act out these activities through dramatic play.

Materials

4 boxes
spring items:
    garden trowel,
    galoshes, rain
    cap
summer items:
    sunglasses, swim
    goggles, beach
    towel
fall items: rake,
    jacket, scarf,
    football
winter items: hat,
    mittens, earmuffs

VOCABULARY

activity   fall   season   spring   summer   weather   winter

PREPARATION

- Assemble one box of spring items, one of summer items, and so on.
- Label the boxes by season.

WHAT TO DO

1. Talk with the children about the differences between the seasons. Explain that each season has different weather and people do different things each season of the year.
2. Ask the children the following questions:
   - What are some things we do in the spring when it rains and flowers bloom?
   - What are some things we do in the summer when it is hot and sunny?
   - What are some things we do in the fall when the leaves change?
   - What are some things we do in the winter when it snows?
3. Divide the children into four groups and give each group one of the boxes.
4. Invite each group to open the boxes and explore their contents. Challenge the children to name the objects and explore them through pretend play.

TEACHER-TO-TEACHER TIP

- Consider rotating the boxes through the groups until all of the groups have used all of the boxes.

ASSESSMENT

To assess the children's learning, consider the following:
- Were the children able to identify the items in the boxes and describe the items' uses?
- Can the children identify the seasons associated with the items?

Sue Bradford Edwards, Florissant, MO

Children's Books

All the Seasons of the Year by Deborah Lee Rose
Circle of Seasons by Gerda Muller
The Reasons for Seasons by Gail Gibbons

Five Little Snowmen

3+

LEARNING OBJECTIVES

The children will:
1. Discuss the differences between the seasons, focusing on winter.
2. Develop their listening skills.
3. Develop their counting skills.

Materials

VOCABULARY

melt   numbers 1–5   season   snowflake   sun   winter

WHAT TO DO

1. On a sunny day in the winter, talk with the children about what the sun does to snow.
2. If possible, point out places where the snow is melting.
3. Talk with the children about how, as the sun comes out and the temperature rises above freezing, the snow begins to melt. Point out that this would include snowmen as well.
4. Recite the following song with the children:

Five Little Snowmen by MaryAnn F. Kohl
Five little snowmen standing in a row,
Each had a hat and a big red bow.
Out came the sun and it shone all day,
One little snowman melted away.
(Additional verses: Repeat the song, reducing the number of snowmen each time.)

ASSESSMENT

To assess the children's learning, consider the following:
- Do the children understand what happens to snow in the sun?
- Can the children count backward from five?

MaryAnn F. Kohl, Bellingham, WA

Children's Books

Snow by Uri Shulevitz
Snowballs by Lois Ehlert
The Snowflake by Neil Waldman
Snowmen at Night by Caralyn Buehner
The Tiny Snowflake by Arthur Ginolfi

Good Morning, Seasons! 3+

LEARNING OBJECTIVES

The children will:
1. Learn a greeting song.
2. Learn the names of the seasons.

Materials

VOCABULARY

fall   greeting   hello   season   spring   summer   winter

WHAT TO DO

1. Talk with the children about the current season of the year. Ask the children what the season feels like in the morning.
2. Challenge the children to identify each season by describing its weather.
3. Teach the children the following greeting song:

    Good Morning, Seasons! by Susan Oldham Hill
    (Tune: "Twinkle, Twinkle, Little Star")
    Good morning, winter! Hello, fall;
    Good morning, seasons, one and all.
    Good morning, summer! Hello, spring;
    Here's a morning song to sing.
    Hello summer, spring, and fall;
    Hello, winter; hello, all!

4. Sing the song with the children in the morning throughout the year.

TEACHER-TO-TEACHER TIP

● Consider having the children suggest actions that indicate the various seasons in the song.

ASSESSMENT

To assess the children's learning, consider the following:
● Can the children identify the seasons by name and describe the kind of weather they have?
● Can the children sing the song?

Susan Oldham Hill, Lakeland, FL

Children's Books

The Reasons for Seasons by Gail Gibbons
Sunshine Makes the Seasons by Franklyn M. Branley
Watching the Seasons by Edana Eckart

I See Snow

3+

The children will:
1. Learn about snow and the winter season.
2. Memorize a fingerplay.
3. Develop their small motor skills.

Materials

VOCABULARY

cold   covering   frosty   season   snow   snowflake   winter

WHAT TO DO

1. During the winter season, gather the children together and discuss the season with them.
2. Ask the children to name features of the winter season. Lead the discussion around to snow. Read the children a book about the snow (see the list to the left for examples).
3. Recite the following fingerplay with the children:

I See Snow by Shyamala Shanmugasundaram
(Tune: "I Hear Thunder")
I see snow. (hold right palm horizontally to forehead)
I see snow. (hold left palm horizontally to forehead)
Look around, look around. (open arms wide)
Small and white snowflakes, (bring thumb and index finger together)
Cold and frosty snowflakes, (pretend to shiver, clenching both fists close to the chest)
Covering the ground. (pretend to pat the ground)

ASSESSMENT

To assess the children's learning, consider the following:
- Can the children identify some features of the winter season?
- Are the children able to act out the fingerplay?

Shyamala Shanmugasundaram, Mumbai, India

Children's Books

The First Day of Winter by Denise Fleming
Snowballs by Lois Ehlert
White Snow, Bright Snow by Alvin Tresselt

I Wish I Were a Little Bluebird

3+

Materials

LEARNING OBJECTIVES

The children will:
1. Learn about the habits of birds in the springtime.
2. Develop their memory skills.
3. Learn a song about birds in spring.

VOCABULARY

bird	egg	father	feather	hatch
mother	nest	season	spring	

WHAT TO DO

1. Talk with the children about springtime. Ask the children what birds do in spring.
2. Teach the children the following song. Encourage the children to make up motions to go along with the various lines of the song.

   I Wish I Were a Little Bluebird by Tina R. Durham-Woehler
   (Tune: Oscar Mayer weiner jingle)
   Oh, I wish I were a little happy bluebird,
   Oh, that is what I'd really like to be.
   For if I were a little happy bluebird,
   Come spring I'd build my nest up in the tree.

   Oh, I wish I were a little baby bluebird.
   Oh, that is what I'd really like to be.
   For if I were a little baby bluebird,
   Come spring I'd hatch from my egg in that tree.

   Oh, I wish I were a mommy bluebird,
   Oh, that is what I'd really like to be.
   For if I were a mommy bluebird,
   Come spring I'd feed worms to my babies in the tree.

ASSESSMENT

To assess the children's learning, consider the following:
- Can the children describe the habits of birds in spring?
- Are the children able to recite the song?
- What kind of actions do the children invent for the various lines of the song?

Tina R. Durham-Woehler, Lebanon, TN

Children's Books

The Best Nest by Doris L. Mueller
From Egg to Robin by Susan Canizares
How and Why Birds Build Nests by Elaine Pascoe, Joel Kupperstein, and Dwight Kuhn
A Nest Full of Eggs by Priscilla Belz Jenkins and Lizzy Rockwell
Owl Babies by Martin Waddell and Patrick Benson
Whose Nest Is This? by Heidi Roemer

In the Seasons

3+

LEARNING OBJECTIVES

The children will:

1. Learn about the differences between the seasons.
2. Develop their memory skills.

Materials

large chart paper
felt-tip marker
laminating materials
stick puppets
   representing
   wind, snow, rain,
   and sun

VOCABULARY

fall   season   spring   summer   winter

PREPARATION

- On the chart paper, print the words to the poem below.
- Laminate the paper and hang the poem on a chart stand in the classroom.

WHAT TO DO

1. Gather the children together and discuss the four seasons. Talk about how each season is different from the others.
2. Show the children the poster with the words to "In the Seasons." Read the poem to the children and then recite it with them.

In the Seasons by Jackie Wright

In the fall,
In the fall,
When the wind blows the leaves
In the fall,
In the fall,
I see leaves fall from the trees.

In the winter,
In the winter,
It gets cold and it can snow.
In the winter,
In the winter,
Oh, how the snow can blow.

In the spring,
In the spring,
When the rain begins to fall
In the spring,
In the spring,
Good times are had by all.

In the summer,
In the summer,
When the sun shines so bright
In the summer,
In the summer,
We play outside day and night.

3. Consider creating stick puppets with images that pertain to the various seasons and inviting the children to wave the appropriate puppets as they recite the different verses of the poem.

ASSESSMENT

To assess the children's learning, consider the following:

- Can the children identify the seasons based on their weather?
- Can the children recite the poem?

Children's Books

Caps, Hats, Socks, and Mittens: A Book About the Four Seasons by Louise Borden
Housekeeper of the Wind by Christine Widman
Sylvester and the Magic Pebble by William Steig

Jackie Wright, Enid, OK

The Lawnmower Song

3+

LEARNING OBJECTIVES

The children will:

1. Learn to sing in high, normal, and deep tones.
2. Develop their large motor skills.

Materials

VOCABULARY

blade   grass   lawn   season   spring   summer

WHAT TO DO

1. Discuss with the children how quickly grass grows in the spring and why people cut their grass. Ask the children if they have family members who regularly cut grass in the spring and summer. Ask the children if they have ever played in very tall grass.

2. Teach the children the following song with all the motions and voice changes:

The Lawnmower Song by Kay Flowers
(Tune: "Here We Go Round the Mulberry Bush")

I'm a little blade of grass, blade of grass, blade of grass. (squat and sing in high voice)
I'm a little blade of grass and in the lawn I'm growing. (begin to stand up)

I'm a taller blade of grass, blade of grass, blade of grass. (stand and sing normally)
I'm a taller blade of grass and in the lawn I'm growing. (raise hands above head)

I'm a great big blade of grass, blade of grass, blade of grass. (stretch arms high overhead and sing in deep voice)
I'm a great big blade of grass. Oh, no! Here comes the lawnmower! (make loud mower sound and squat back down)

I'm a little blade of grass, blade of grass, blade of grass. (squat and sing in high voice)
I'm a little blade of grass and in the lawn I'm growing.

Children's Books

Larry the Lawnmower by Jeanne Archambault
Pinky and the Runaway Lawnmower by Bridget Jardine
Stanley Mows the Lawn by Craig Frazier

ASSESSMENT

To assess the children's learning, consider the following:

- Can the children move their bodies from a squat to a full stretch and back to a squat?
- Can the children change their voices to sing high, normally, and in a deep tone?

Kay Flowers, Summerfield, OH

The Seasons Song

3+

LEARNING OBJECTIVES

The children will:
1. Develop their vocabularies.
2. Learn about what makes the seasons distinct.
3. Explore the meanings of letters and images.

Materials

chart paper
marker

VOCABULARY

cold	cool	fall	freezing	hot	rain
season	snow	spring	summer	sunny	warm

WHAT TO DO

1. Engage the children in a discussion about the seasons. Ask the children what each season feels and looks like. Challenge the children to think of various terms that describe characteristics of the seasons. Write these terms down on a sheet of chart paper, separating them by season.
2. Tell the children they are going to play a game called "Seasons."
3. Recite the following rhyme to the children. After each verse, challenge the children to say the name of the season the verse describes.

The Seasons Song by Anonymous

It's hot outside!
Let's go to the lake.
What a lot of splashing
Our jumping in will make!

Brr! I'm so chilly.
Look at all this snow!
Let's put on coats and scarves
And a-sledding we will go!

It's starting to get cool outside.
Leaves are blowing all around
In lots of pretty colors.
*Let's rake them into piles on the
    ground.*

The birds are coming back.
The flowers are starting to bloom.
Listen to the rain and thunder
Go trickle and ka-boom!

4. After the children identify the season described by each verse, ask the children how they figured out the correct season.

ASSESSMENT

To assess the children's learning, consider the following:
● Can the children associate various terms and ideas with specific seasons?
● Can the children identify the seasons described in the different verses of the rhyme?

Children's Books

Our Seasons by Ranida T. McKneally and Grace Lin
The Reasons for Seasons by Gail Gibbons
Watching the Seasons by Edana Eckart

Carol Hupp, Farmersville, IL

Shiver When It Snows

3+

LEARNING OBJECTIVES

The children will:

1. Learn about the seasons, focusing on winter.
2. Develop their memory skills.
3. Learn a song about the winter weather.

Materials

VOCABULARY

cold   ice   quiver   season   shiver   snow   winter

WHAT TO DO

1. On a particularly cold winter day, gather the children together and discuss the weather with them.
2. Ask the children if the weather is similar in the summer.
3. Talk with the children about how the weather makes them feel. Are they cold? Do they shiver?
4. Invite the children to stand up and recite the following song, acting out the words as they sing it:

Shiver When It Snows by MaryAnn F. Kohl
(Tune: "If You're Happy and You Know It")
Oh, you shiver and you quiver when it snows,
Oh, you shiver and you quiver when it snows,
Your hands feel just like ice,
So you rub them once or twice.
YES, you shiver and you quiver when it snows.
BRRRRRRRRRRRRR!!!

5. Talk with the children about how moving around can help them to stay warm in the winter.

ASSESSMENT

To assess the children's learning, consider the following:

● Can the children distinguish between the winter and other seasons?
● Are the children able to recite and act out the song?

Children's Books

Snow by Uri Shulevitz
Snowballs by Lois Ehlert
The Snowflake by Neil Waldman
Snowmen at Night by Caralyn Buehner
The Tiny Snowflake by Arthur Ginolfi

MaryAnn F. Kohl, Bellingham, WA

Snowflakes and Cakes

3+

LEARNING OBJECTIVES

The children will:
1. Discuss the differences between the seasons, focusing on winter.
2. Develop their listening skills.
3. Memorize and recite a poem.

Materials

poster board
marker

VOCABULARY

cake   cookie   season   snowflake   winter

WHAT TO DO

1. Gather the children together and discuss the seasons with them. Ask them to describe the winter season in particular.
2. Ask the children to think of words that describe the winter season.
3. Write down the children's words on the poster board.
4. Ask the children what they wish snow tasted like. Listen to their responses.
5. Recite and act out the following winter-related poem with the children:

Snowflakes and Cakes by MaryAnn F. Kohl
If all the snowflakes
Were cookies and cakes
Oh, what a snow it would be!
I'd go outside
With my mouth open wide (open mouth and stick out tongue)
Ah, ah, ah, ah, ah, ah, ah!
If all of the snowflakes
Were cookies and cakes
Oh, what a snow it would be!

6. Repeat the poem with the children, inviting them to imagine new flavors for the snow.

ASSESSMENT

To assess the children's learning, consider the following:
- Can the children differentiate between the various seasons?
- Can the children remember and repeat the song?

Children's Books

Snow by Uri Shulevitz
Snowballs by Lois Ehlert
The Snowflake by Neil Waldman
Snowmen at Night by Caralyn Buehner
The Tiny Snowflake by Arthur Ginolfi

MaryAnn F. Kohl, Bellingham, WA

All the Little Colored Leaves

4+

Materials

scissors (adult use only)
construction paper in fall colors
outlines of various leaves

LEARNING OBJECTIVES

The children will:
1. Learn to identify colors by name.
2. Develop their listening skills.
3. Recite a rhyme together.

VOCABULARY

brown   fall   green   leaf   red   yellow

PREPARATION

● Cut out construction paper leaves. Make at least one per child.

WHAT TO DO

1. Gather the children together and talk with them about how leaves fall in autumn.
2. Give each child a paper leaf. Ask the children what kind of sounds the wind makes. Talk with the children about how the wind helps the leaves to fall.
3. Ask the children to gather in a circle and hold up their leaves.
4. Recite the following poem with the children:

All the Little Colored Leaves by Anne Houghton
Many little colored leaves hanging on a tree,
Red leaves, yellow leaves want to fall free.
The wind comes whooshing through the town (children say "whoosh")
And suddenly the _____ leaves flutter down; (say a color of leaf; children holding a leaf of that color drop their leaves)
Now all the little _____ leaves are on the ground.
(Repeat until all the leaves are on the ground.)

5. In addition to dropping the leaves, invite the children to perform the action of leaves falling when their colors are called.

TEACHER-TO-TEACHER TIP

● Consider having children with well-developed small motor skills cut out the leaf shapes at the start of the activity, using child-safe scissors.

ASSESSMENT

To assess the children's learning, consider the following:
● Can the children recognize colors by name?
● Can the children drop their leaves at the appropriate times?

Anne Houghton, Melbourne, Victoria, Australia

Children's Books

Autumn by Gerda Muller
I Know It's Autumn by Eileen Spinelli
It's Fall by Linda Glaser

It's Hard to Be a Season

4+

LEARNING OBJECTIVES

The children will:

1. Learn the names of the seasons.
2. Recognize the seasons by the changes that take place.
3. Categorize seasonal objects.

Materials

items used during
   the seasons
drawing paper
crayons

VOCABULARY

bathing suit	fall	leaf	season	sled
spring	summer	sweater	winter	

WHAT TO DO

1. Read the children a book about the seasons (see the list to the left). Talk with the children about the seasons, and how they differ.
2. Teach the children the names of the seasons. Ask the children what they like best about each season.
3. Recite the following rhyme with the children:

   It's Hard to Be a Season by Carol L. Levy
   It's hard to be a season
   'Cause you're changing all the time.
   Do I need a sweater?
   Will a bathing suit be better?
   Should I take my sled?
   Put a hat on my head?
   Sweep up the leaves
   Or grow new trees?
   I wish I could always be the same
   Swim and ice-skate
   Never changing my NAME.

4. Talk with the children about how, in some parts of the country, the changes between the seasons are less noticeable. Ask the children if they have ever gone to the beach in the winter, or seen snow in the summer.

Children's Books

Four Seasons Make a Year by Anne Rockwell
The Seasons of Arnold's Apple Tree by Gail Gibbons
Sunshine Makes the Seasons by Franklyn Branley

ASSESSMENT

To assess the children's learning, consider the following:

- Can the children identify the seasons based on descriptions of weather?
- Can the children recite the rhyme?

Carol L. Levy, Woodbury, NY

Leaves in the Fall

4+

LEARNING OBJECTIVES

The children will:

1. Learn about what happens to leaves in the fall.
2. Memorize a simple poem about leaves.

Materials

VOCABULARY

autumn	color	fall	green	large	leaf
orange	red	size	small	sort	

WHAT TO DO

1. Read the children a book about leaves and the fall (see the list to the left for examples). Talk with the children about why some leaves turn colors in the fall while others stay green.
2. Teach the children the following poem. Encourage the children to create actions that go along with each line:

Leaves Are Falling by Shirley Anne Ramaley
Leaves are falling all around,
Some have landed on the ground.

Red, green, and orange I see.
Colors bright as they can be.

I pick one up and take a look.
It's like a picture in my book.

3. As the children recite the poem, encourage them to look for objects that match the colors they mention.

Children's Books

Fall Leaves by Mary Packard
The Leaves Fall All Around by Steve Mack
Leaves in Fall by Martha E. Rustad
Scholastic Science Readers: Fall Leaves Change Colors by Kathleen Weidner Zoehfeld

ASSESSMENT

To assess the children's learning, consider the following:

- Do the children understand why leaves fall in the autumn?
- Can the children recite the poem?

Shirley Anne Ramaley, Sun City, AZ

Lyrical Seasons

4+

LEARNING OBJECTIVES

The children will:
1. Increase their vocabulary.
2. Explore language.
3. Learn to distinguish between the seasons.

Materials

VOCABULARY

fall   leaf   orange   snow   spring   summer   sun   winter

WHAT TO DO

1. Talk with the children about the different seasons. Ask them to describe what each season is like.
2. Recite the following rhyme with the children:

   The Four Seasons by Anonymous
   The winter can be so snowy.
   Springtime is all wet and blowy.
   In summer the sun shines so showy.
   And in fall the leaves have an orange glowy.

3. After reciting the rhyme with the children, ask the children to think of other terms that describe the various seasons.

TEACHER-TO-TEACHER TIP
● With older children, consider introducing the word "adjective."

ASSESSMENT

To assess the children's learning, consider the following:
● Can the children distinguish between the various seasons of the year?
● Can the children think of words to describe each season?

Anna Adeney, Hereford, United Kingdom

Children's Books

Our Seasons by Ranida T. McKneally and Grace Lin
The Reasons for Seasons by Gail Gibbons
Watching the Seasons by Edana Eckart

Let's Build a Snowman

LEARNING OBJECTIVES

The children will:
1. Discuss the weather in the winter season.
2. Learn about snowmen.
3. Develop their large motor skills.

Materials

VOCABULARY

body   carrot   head   nose   snowball   snowman

WHAT TO DO

1. On a snowy day in winter, engage the children in a discussion about the weather. Ask the children if they remember seeing snow like this in the summer.
2. Ask the children to describe the snow, and talk about its accumulation.
3. Ask the children if they have ever seen or built a snowman.
4. Invite the children to sing the following song. Encourage them to make up actions that go along with each verse:

Let's Build a Snowman by Jackie Wright
(Tune: "Let's Build a House")

Let's build a snowman.
Let's build a snowman.
Let's build a snowman.
And work, work, work.

Roll a large snowball.
Roll a large snowball.
Roll a large snowball.
For his body.

Roll a medium snowball.
Roll a medium snowball.

Roll a medium snowball.
For his middle.

Roll a small snowball.
Roll a small snowball.
Roll a small snowball.
For his head.

Now add a carrot.
Now add a carrot.
Now add a carrot
For his nose.

Now add a scarf.
Now add a scarf.
Now add a scarf.
Around his neck.

Don't forget the hat.
Don't forget the hat.
Don't forget the hat.
For his head.

(Additional Verses: Encourage the children to make up more verses for the song.)

TEACHER-TO-TEACHER TIP

● Consider bringing the children outside to work on making small snowmen if there is space and sufficient snow available.

ASSESSMENT

To assess the children's learning, consider the following:
● Can the children distinguish between winter and other seasons?
● Are the children able to recite the song?

Children's Books

Sadie and the Snowman by Allen Morgan
Snowballs by Lois Ehlert
The Snowman by Raymond Briggs

Jackie Wright, Enid, OK

Spring Day

4+

LEARNING OBJECTIVES

The children will:
1. Differentiate springtime from other seasons.
2. Develop their memory skills.
3. Recite a song.

Materials

VOCABULARY

bat   cap   day   kite   play   spring

WHAT TO DO

1. Gather the children together and engage them in a discussion about springtime.
2. Ask the children how spring is different from other seasons of the year. Ask if it snows in the springtime, or if the springtime is when people go to the beach.
3. Encourage the children to name some of their favorite springtime activities.
4. With the children, sing the following song:

Spring Day by Jackie Wright
(Tune: "Hickory Dickory Dock")
It is a lovely spring day!
I'm on my way to play!
I grab my cap,
And next my bat,
And then I am on my way!

(Invite the children to make up verses for other springtime activities)

It is a lovely spring day!
I'm on my way to play!
I fly my kite
With all my might,
And then I am on my way!

ASSESSMENT

To assess the children's learning, consider the following:
- Can the children describe particular activities they like to do in spring?
- Are the children able to recite the song? Can they make up new verses?

Jackie Wright, Enid, OK

Children's Books

It's Spring by Linda Glaser
My Spring Robin by Anne Rockwell
One Bright Monday Morning by Arline and Joseph Baum
When Spring Comes by Robert Maass

There Once Was a Caterpillar

4+

Materials

LEARNING OBJECTIVES

The children will:
1. Learn about the life stages of a butterfly.
2. Develop their memory recall.
3. Recite a fingerplay.
4. Develop their small motor skills.

VOCABULARY

butterfly   caterpillar   chrysalis   cocoon   spring

WHAT TO DO

1. Talk with the children about caterpillars and butterflies. Ask the children if they have seen butterflies outside, and if they know what the butterflies were doing. Talk about how butterflies only come out in the spring and summer, and that before they are butterflies, they are caterpillars.

2. Teach the children the following fingerplay:

There Once Was a Caterpillar by Ingelore Mix
In June a caterpillar on a leaf once sat. (put left-hand palm upward)
It ate and ate and ate 'til it got fat, (place forefinger of other hand on top of palm)
Then covered itself in silk of green (close hand to cover forefinger)
Never, ever again to be seen.
Magic took place, I do not lie,
The caterpillar turned into a butterfly. (put both hands together, palms facing outward)
So pretty it was I wished it stayed
But it opened its wings and flew away. (open up hands so that the thumbs touch each other)
I said good-bye because I know
It is on its journey to Mexico. (move fingers up and down in a flying motion)

ASSESSMENT

To assess the children's learning, consider the following:
- Do the children understand the butterfly's life cycle?
- Can the children repeat the fingerplay?

Ingelore Mix, Amherst, NH

Children's Books

Charlie the Caterpillar by Dom Deluise
Clara Caterpillar by Pamela Duncan Edwards
Nature's Children: Monarch Butterfly by Bill Ivy
The Very Hungry Caterpillar by Eric Carle

Winter Clothing Song

4+

LEARNING OBJECTIVES

The children will:
1. Learn about season-appropriate winter clothing.
2. Recite a fingerplay.
3. Think of new verses for the fingerplay.

Materials

VOCABULARY

boot   hat   jacket   mitten   scarf   snow   winter

WHAT TO DO

1. Talk with the children about the weather in the winter season. Ask the children what kinds of clothes are appropriate for the winter.

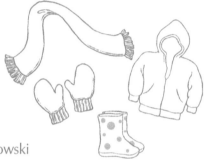

2. Recite the following fingerplay with the children:

   Winter Clothing Song by Kaethe Lewandowski
   (Tune: "She'll Be Coming 'Round the Mountain")
   I'll be wearing two warm mittens when it snows. (clap, clap)
   I'll be wearing two warm mittens when it snows. (clap, clap)
   I'll be wearing two warm mittens, I'll be wearing two warm mittens,
   I'll be wearing two warm mittens when it snows.

   Additional verses
   ...two warm boots... (stomp, stomp)
   ...one warm hat... (pat, pat)
   ...one warm jacket... (zip, zip)
   ...one warm scarf... (ahh, ahh)

3. Challenge the children to come up with additional verses and actions for this fingerplay.

ASSESSMENT

To assess the children's learning, consider the following:
- Can the children name winter-appropriate clothing?
- Can the children recite the fingerplay and think of new verses and actions for it?

Kaethe Lewandowski, Centreville, VA

Children's Books

All You Need for a Snowman by Alice Schertle
Friendly Snowman by Sharon Gordon
The Jacket I Wear in the Snow by Shirley Neitzel
Our Snowman by M.B. Goffstein
The Snowman by Raymond Briggs
Snowmen at Night by Caralyn Buehner
Thomas' Snowsuit by Robert Munsch

Winter Snowflakes

4+

LEARNING OBJECTIVES

The children will:

1. Learn about how snowflakes are made and where they come from.
2. Develop their vocabulary.
3. Learn a verse about snowflakes.

Materials

paper
scissors (adult use
  only)

Children's Books

Millions of Snowflakes
  by Mary McKenna
Siddals and Elizabeth
  Sayles
*The Secret Life of a
Snowflake: An Up-Close
Look at the Art and
Science of Snowflakes*
by Kenneth Libbrecht
Winter's First Snowflake
by Cheri L. Hallwood

VOCABULARY

cold   season   six (sides)   snowflake   weather   winter

PREPARATION

● Cut out a few snowflake shapes and decorate the room with them.

WHAT TO DO

1. Talk with the children about snowflakes. Ask the children if they have seen snow falling before, and whether they have seen a single snowflake up close. Ask the children to describe the shape of the snowflake.
2. Point out the hanging snowflake cutouts in the classroom and have the children describe their shapes.
3. Teach the children the following fingerplay:

Winter Snowflakes by Shirley Anne Ramaley
Snow is falling on the ground. (hold fingers high, imitate snow
    falling)
I can see it all around. (look all around the room)
I watch the snowflakes as they land. (look on the floor or ground)
And one sets down right on my hand. (look at a hand...and
    SMILE!)

ASSESSMENT

To assess the children's learning, consider the following:
● Can the children describe the shapes of snowflakes?
● Are the children able to recite the fingerplay and make the appropriate motions?

Shirley Anne Ramaley, Sun City, AZ

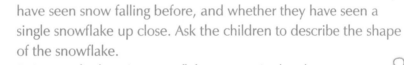

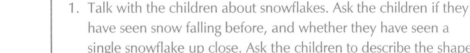

What Do We Use in the Rain?

5+

Materials

LEARNING OBJECTIVES

The children will:
1. Learn about spring rains.
2. Develop their literacy skills.

VOCABULARY

boot   glove   rain   rain hat   raincoat   spring   umbrella

WHAT TO DO

1. Gather the children together and talk with them about the rain. Explain that the springtime is often a very rainy part of the year.
2. Ask the children what kinds of items they would wear and use if they were outside in the rain.
3. Teach the children the following song:

What Do We Use in the Rain? by Jackie Wright
(Tune: "Mary Had a Little Lamb")
What do we use in the rain,
In the rain, in the rain?
What do we use in the rain,
To keep from getting wet?

We use _____ in the rain,
In the rain, in the rain.
We use _____ in the rain
To keep from getting wet.

(Repeat the second verse, challenging children to name other rain-appropriate items.)

ASSESSMENT

To assess the children's learning, consider the following:
- Can the children describe the kind of weather typical in the springtime?
- Can the children name a month that falls in the spring season?
- Can the children name items they would use in the rain?

Jackie Wright, Enid, OK

Children's Books

Amy Loves the Rain by Julia Hoban
Drip Drop by Sharon Gordon
In the Rain with Baby Duck by Amy Hest

Matching Mittens

LEARNING OBJECTIVES

The children will:
1. Compare and match mitten pairs.
2. Develop their small motor skills.

Materials

real mittens or
   mittens cut from
   different colors
   of construction
   paper (1 pair per
   child)
long piece of yarn
   or clothesline
clothespins

VOCABULARY

cold   different   match   mitten   same   season   winter

PREPARATION
- Precut the mitten shapes if necessary.
- Hang the clothesline in the room at a low enough height for the children to reach. Clip the clothespins to the line.
- Hide one mitten from each pair of mittens around the room.

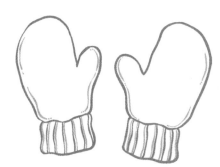

WHAT TO DO
1. During the winter season, read the children a book about mittens (see the list to the left). Talk with the children about how mittens help keep hands warm in the winter.
2. Show the children the clothesline and the unhidden halves of the mitten sets.
3. Give each child one of the remaining mittens from the pairs and invite the children to hunt for their matching mittens.
4. Once the children find their matching mittens, help the children pin them to the clothesline. (**Note:** Working with clothespins is a great small motor activity.)
5. Repeat the game as often as desired, giving the children new mittens to match.

TEACHER-TO-TEACHER TIP
- For children who may have trouble with this activity, consider practicing matching up the mittens before hiding them.

Children's Books

The Missing Mitten Mystery by Steven Kellogg
The Mitten by Jan Brett
The Mitten Tree by Candace Christiansen

ASSESSMENT
To assess the children's learning, consider the following:
- Can the children match their mittens to those hidden around the room?
- Can the children pin their mittens to the clothesline?

Sandra Ryan, Buffalo, NY

Seasons Match

LEARNING OBJECTIVES

The children will:
1. Learn the names of the four seasons.
2. Develop their small motor skills.
3. Learn to associate objects with specific seasons.

Materials

card stock
felt-tip marker
collection of
    seasonal pictures
sticky-backed
    Velcro©

VOCABULARY

autumn   fall   spring   summer   winter

PREPARATION

- On card stock, make eight lotto boards, two for each season. Write the names of the seasons at the tops of each board.
- Make a grid on the boards with between four and 12 squares.
- Put a season-appropriate picture in each square, making photocopies of those images. Cut out the photocopied images.
- Laminate the lotto boards and individual photocopied images.

Spring Lotto

WHAT TO DO

1. Talk with the children about the seasons, asking them to describe the seasons and things that remind them of the seasons.
2. Show the children the boards and individual image cards.
3. Invite the children to take turns with the different boards, identifying the seasons by name, and then searching through the individual image cards for those that match the seasons.

ASSESSMENT

To assess the children's learning, consider the following:
- Can the children identify and differentiate between the seasons?
- Can the children match seasonal images to the correct seasons?

Jackie Wright, Enid, OK

Children's Books

Four Seasons Make a Year by Anne Rockwell
The House of Four Seasons by Roger Duvoisin
The Little House by Virginia Lee Burton

Mixed-Up Seasons Relay

4+

LEARNING OBJECTIVES

The children will:
1. Learn about how the weather affects what we decide to wear.
2. Develop their large motor skills.
3. Practice following directions.
4. Support one another.

Materials

multiple articles of clothing appropriate for each of the different seasons

tape

VOCABULARY

cold   fall   spring   summer   sun   weather   wind   winter

PREPARATION

- Use tape to mark four start and end lines for the relay race. Put a pile of seasonal clothing at the starting line for each team.

WHAT TO DO

1. Talk with the children about how the season's weather affects how people dress.
2. Discuss how clothing can help protect people from cold, rain, sun, and wind.
3. Divide the children into four groups.
4. Have each team line up behind one season's pile of clothing.
5. The children in each group take turns running the course. To do so, each of the children must:
   - Say the name of the season line they are standing in;
   - Put on all of the clothing in the season's pile, naming the items as they put them on;
   - Run to (or beyond) the end line, turn around, and return to the starting line; and
   - Remove the seasonal clothes and pass them to the next person in line.

Note: Rather than make this a competitive activity, simply have the groups of children move from one season to the next season, and encourage them to celebrate one another as they complete each race.

ASSESSMENT

To assess the children's learning, consider the following:
- Are the children able to follow directions?
- Are the children able to dress themselves?
- Do the children support one another as they run?

Children's Books

All Around the Seasons by Barney Saltzberg
The Reasons for Seasons by Gail Gibbons
What Makes the Seasons? by Megan Montague Cash

Janet Hammond, Mount Laurel, NJ

Season Folders

LEARNING OBJECTIVES

The children will:
1. Differentiate between the seasons.
2. Develop their ability to see images as symbols.

Materials

old file folders
marker
collection of
pictures of
seasonal activities
glue stick

VOCABULARY

fall   season   spring   summer   winter

PREPARATION

● Write a season's name inside each file folder. On the front of each, glue a picture representing the season.

WHAT TO DO

1. Begin by talking with the children about the seasons. Ask the children what people do and wear during the different seasons.
2. Ask four children to come to the front of the class. Give each of the children a folder.
3. Invite those children to peak inside their folders to see what season folder they are holding, but ask them not to tell the other children.
4. Hand out seasonal images to the other children.
5. Challenge the children in the class to take turns identifying the activities on their cards and then naming the seasons in which people normally do those activities.
6. The children then bring their images up to the children at the front of the class and put the images in the correct folders, saying the names of the seasons as they do so.

ASSESSMENT

To assess the children's learning, consider the following:
● Can the children describe activities that people do in the various seasons?
● Can the children identify which images belong in which folders?

Jackie Wright, Enid, OK

Children's Books

All Around the Seasons by Barney Saltzberg
Our Seasons by Ranida T. McKneally and Grace Lin
The Reasons for Seasons by Gail Gibbons
Watching the Seasons by Edana Eckart

Colorful Umbrellas

4+

LEARNING OBJECTIVES

The children will:
1. Learn about springtime weather.
2. Learn to identify colors by name.
3. Begin to develop their literacy skills.

Materials

images of umbrellas of different colors
scissors (adult use only)
white construction paper
markers of various colors
laminator (optional)

VOCABULARY

puddle   rain   season   spring   umbrella   weather

PREPARATION

- Cut out (or draw) and attach to construction paper images of umbrellas of various colors. Print the names of the colors on separate pieces of construction paper. **Note:** It is best to write the names of the colors in those colors.
- Laminate both the image and word cards for durability.

WHAT TO DO

1. On a rainy day in spring, gather the children together and discuss the weather. Ask if any of the children used umbrellas on their way to the class that day. Explain that the springtime is often rainy.
2. Show the children the images of umbrellas, and talk about the different colors.
3. Show the children the matching word cards. Spell out the names of the colors for the children.
4. Challenge the children to match the word cards to the umbrella cards by color. Also challenge the children to spell the names of the colors.

ASSESSMENT

To assess the children's learning, consider the following:
- Can the children identify the colors of the umbrellas by name?
- Can the children match the umbrella cards to the color-name cards?
- Can the children spell the names of the colors?

Jackie Wright, Enid, OK

Children's Books

Ella's Umbrellas by Jennifer Lloyd
The Red Umbrella by Christina Gonzalez
The Umbrella by Jan Brett

Getting Dressed: "The Know-How!"

4+

LEARNING OBJECTIVES

The children will:
1. Learn about season-appropriate clothing.
2. Learn to follow steps.
3. Develop their small motor skills.

construction paper
markers
paint and brushes
images of people in
    season-
    appropriate
    clothing
small adult-sized or
    large child-sized
    swimming trunks,
    sweaters, pants,
    raincoats, winter
    coats, and so on

VOCABULARY

boot   change   dressing   hat   next step   season   umbrella   weather

PREPARATION

● Make charts that show the steps of getting dressed in clothes appropriate for each season.

WHAT TO DO

1. Gather the children together and talk with them about how they got dressed that morning. Ask the children if they chose their clothes. Ask the children why they picked the clothes they did.
2. Show the children the various articles of clothing, and challenge them to identify the seasons appropriate for each.
3. Set up the charts of the steps involved in getting dressed for each season, setting the season-appropriate clothing out before the charts. Invite the children to take turns following the steps and getting dressed for each season.

SONG

I Know How to Dress Myself by Eileen Lucas
I know how to dress myself.
I know how to dress myself.
I don't need your help, I don't need your help.
I know how to dress myself.

Children's Books

Bing: Get Dressed by Ted Dewan
Getting Dressed by Felicity Brooks
Naked Mole Rat Gets Dressed by Mo Willems

ASSESSMENT

To assess the children's learning, consider the following:
● Can the children identify clothing that is appropriate for each season?
● Are the children able to follow the steps to put on the correct clothing in each season?

Eileen Lucas, Fort McMurray, Alberta, Canada

Harvest Time Memory Cards

4+

Materials

5–10 pictures of various fruits and vegetables
3" x 5" cards
glue
marker

LEARNING OBJECTIVES

The children will:
1. Learn about harvesting various crops.
2. Develop their comparison and matching skills.

VOCABULARY

crop   fruit   grow   harvest   ripe   season   shuck   vegetable

PREPARATION

● Glue individual pictures of the various crops on 3" x 5" cards.
● Write the name of each crop on other 3" x 5" cards.

WHAT TO DO

1. Talk with the children about growing and harvesting food. Explain that people typically plant this produce in the spring season, that it grows in the summer, and that the fruits and vegetables get ripe and ready to pick in the fall, when it is time to harvest them.

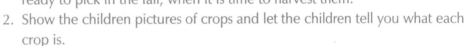

2. Show the children pictures of crops and let the children tell you what each crop is.
3. Place the name of the crop beside its picture. Demonstrate how to harvest each crop and let the children imitate the motions (shucking corn, picking apples, carrying heavy pumpkins, and so on).
4. Mix up the picture and word cards. Let the children try to match them up and show the method of harvesting each crop.
5. This activity can be made progressively more challenging by adding new cards as the children successfully match the old cards.

TEACHER-TO-TEACHER TIP

● Consider visiting a pumpkin patch or apple orchard during the fall harvest season.

ASSESSMENT

To assess the children's learning, consider the following:
● Can the children match words to the pictures?
● Do the children differentiate between the methods of harvesting crops?

Children's Books

Fall Harvest by Gail Saunders-Smith
Harvest Time by Mercer Mayer
Why Do Leaves Change Color? by Betsy Maestro

Kay Flowers, Summerfield, OH

Life of a Tree

4+

LEARNING OBJECTIVES

The children will:
1. Learn the stages of a tree's life.
2. Become aware of the world around them.

brown construction
    paper
tape
tree branches
    (optional)
artificial leaves in
    fall, spring, and
    summer colors
brown yarn
sentence strips

VOCABULARY

bark	blossom	branch	bud	chlorophyll
evergreen	fruit	leaf	stem	tree

PREPARATION

- Clear a section of the classroom wall where the class tree will "grow."
- Start the class tree by attaching a brown construction paper sapling or small tree to the wall at floor level.

WHAT TO DO

1. Engage the children in a discussion about how trees change through the course of the year. Ask the children to describe the different things they have noticed about trees at different times of the year.
2. Tell the children they will be making a classroom tree.
3. Show the children the sapling or small tree.
4. Give the children lengths of yarn to make larger "roots" for the sapling. Attach sentence strips next to the sapling and "roots," writing the names of those sections on the cards.
5. Invite the children to use more construction paper and yarn to make a larger trunk, limbs, and so on, asking the children to name those parts of the tree as they work. Label these sections of the tree with sentence strips as the children work.
6. According to the season, invite the children to add or change the leaves on the tree. Leave this tree up throughout the year and periodically refer to it when discussing weather and the seasons.

Children's Books

I Am a Leaf by Jean
    Marzollo
Leaves by David Ezra
    Stein
Red Leaf, Yellow Leaf by
    Lois Ehlert

ASSESSMENT

To assess the children's learning, consider the following:
- Can the children identify the season according to how the tree is decorated?
- Can the children identify the various parts of the tree by name?

Holly Dzierzanowski, Brenham, TX

My Favorite Words

4+

LEARNING OBJECTIVES

The children will:

1. Learn the names of the four seasons.
2. Develop their small motor and vocabulary skills.
3. Identify seasonal pictures and words.

Materials

4 large sheets of
   card stock
washable felt-tip
   marker
laminating materials
collection of
   seasonal pictures
tape or gummy
   adhesive

VOCABULARY

| autumn | fall | leaf | pumpkin | rain | season |
| snow | spring | summer | sun | umbrella | winter |

PREPARATION

- On four separate sheets of card stock, write "My Favorite (Season's Name) Words."
- Laminate the posters.

WHAT TO DO

1. Talk with the children about the four seasons. Ask the children to think of things that remind them of the seasons.
2. Show the children the different seasonal posters and the various seasonal images.
3. Invite the children to match the seasonal images to the correct season posters. Help the children to attach the images to the posters.
4. Ask the children to name the items they are putting on the poster. The children can use a washable felt-tip marker to write the names of the objects beside their images.
5. Leave out the poster for the current season, and let the children add images to it over time.
6. Change the poster when the season changes. Consider leaving the two posters up and having the children compare the similarities and differences between them.

Children's Books

Sleepy Bear by Lydia
   Dabcovich
Snowballs by Lois Ehlert
When Autumn Comes
   by Robert Maass

ASSESSMENT

To assess the children's learning, consider the following:

- Can the children identify objects that relate to a specific season?
- Can the children describe the similarities and differences between two seasons?

Jackie Wright, Enid, OK

S-P-R-I-N-G

4+

LEARNING OBJECTIVES

The children will:
1. Identify each letter in the word "spring."
2. Find pictures of objects and things whose names begin with the letters of the word "spring."

Materials

child-safe scissors
glue
poster board
magazines (for younger children, you may want to have pictures already cut out that begin with the letters S-P-R-I-N-G)

VOCABULARY

alphabet	beginning sound	letter
match	season	spring

PREPARATION

- Write the letters S-P-R-I-N-G at the top of a piece of poster board, leaving 3"—4" between letters.
- Draw a line from the top of the poster board to the bottom between letters.

WHAT TO DO

1. Introduce the children to the word "spring." Help the children identify each letter and the sound of each letter. Challenge the children to think of words that begin with those letters.
2. Set out the magazines and child-safe scissors. Explain to the children that they will look for pictures of things whose names begin with those sounds.
3. When the children find an image of an object whose name begins with one of the letters' sounds, help the children glue the image on the poster board under the correct letter.

TEACHER-TO-TEACHER TIP

- Make different posters each season of the year.

ASSESSMENT

To assess the children's learning, consider the following:
- Can the children identify the letters in the word "spring"?
- Can the children name words that begin with the letters in the word "spring"?
- Can the children find images of objects whose names start with the letters in the word "spring" and glue them to the correct spot on the poster board?

Children's Books

The Boy Who Didn't Believe in Spring by Lucille Clifton
Clifford's Spring Clean-Up by Norman Bridwell
Mouse's First Spring by Lauren Thompson

Suzanne Sanders Maxymuk, Cherry Hill, NJ

The Scarecrow Sees

LEARNING OBJECTIVES

The children will:

1. Learn about scarecrows and harvests.
2. Develop their small motor skills.

Materials

picture of a
   scarecrow's face
markers and
   crayons
paper
photocopier
crayons

VOCABULARY

autumn	crop	fall	harvest
scarecrow	season	weather	

PREPARATION

- At the top of a sheet of paper, write, "The scarecrow sees a..." using a picture of a scarecrow's face instead of the word "scarecrow." Be sure to leave lots of space at the bottom of the page.
- Make several copies of the page.

WHAT TO DO

1. On a fall day, gather the children together and talk with them about how farmers often harvest their crops in the autumn.
2. Explain that farmers often put up scarecrows in their fields to keep birds and other creatures away.
3. Ask the children what things they think a scarecrow might see in a field in autumn.
4. Set out the sheets of paper, along with markers and crayons, and invite the children to draw images of things a scarecrow might see in the field.
5. Help the children write the names of the things they have drawn on their sheets of paper.

ASSESSMENT

To assess the children's learning, consider the following:

- Do the children understand the function of scarecrows?
- What images do the children draw?
- Are the children able to write the names of the objects they drew?

Children's Books

Autumn by Gerda
   Muller
I Know It's Autumn by
   Eileen Spinelli
It's Fall by Linda Glaser

Jackie Wright, Enid, OK

What to Wear on a Rainy Day

5+

Materials

card stock or large
   chart paper
marker
picture of a rain
   cloud
5 images of
   children wearing
   rain gear
5 images of
   children wearing
   clothes
   unsuitable for the
   rain

LEARNING OBJECTIVES

The children will:
1. Learn about spring rains.
2. Develop their literacy skills.

VOCABULARY

boot   glove   rain   rain hat   raincoat   umbrella

PREPARATION

● At the top of the sheet of paper, make a box with the question "What to Wear on a Rainy Day?"
● In the center of the paper, make a large circle. Glue the picture of the rain cloud there, and draw five lines out from the circle.

WHAT TO DO

1. Ask the children to gather in a group on the floor. Talk with the children about how spring is often a rainy part of the year. Ask the children if they can remember rainy days in spring. Mention the saying "April showers bring May flowers."
2. Show the children the "What to Wear on a Rainy Day?" sheet, as well as the images of children wearing clothes that are good and bad to wear in the rain.
3. Challenge the children to choose the images that show clothing good to wear in a spring rain. Ask the children to name those articles of clothing.
4. As the children identify the correct articles of clothing, write the names of the clothing on the chart, and attach the images to the chart as well. Spell out each name for the children, and ask them to repeat the letters and the names.

ASSESSMENT

To assess the children's learning, consider the following:
● Do the children understand that the spring can be an especially rainy time of the year?
● Can the children identify and name weather-appropriate clothing?

Children's Books

Amy Loves the Rain by
   Julia Hoban
Drip Drop by Sharon
   Gordon
*In the Rain with Baby
   Duck* by Amy Hest

Jackie Wright, Enid, OK

Snowflakes in the Parachute

Materials

paper snowflakes
large parachute

LEARNING OBJECTIVES

The children will:
1. Learn to follow directions.
2. Develop their ability to work as a group.
3. Develop their large motor skills.

VOCABULARY

down	high	low	season
snowflake	under	up	winter

PREPARATION

- Cut out several paper snowflakes before this activity.

WHAT TO DO

1. Read the children a book about snowflakes (see list to the left for suggestions).
2. Talk with the children about snowflakes and how they fall.
3. Show the children the parachute, and ask them to help lay it out flat on the ground.
4. Ask the children to stand around the outside of the parachute, hold it with both hands, and lift it into the air.
5. Take out the snowflakes and toss them into the parachute. Invite the children to shake the parachute to make the snowflakes dance.
6. Challenge the children by having them move to the left or right while making the snowflakes fall. Or have the children make the snowflakes jump slightly or jump very high.
7. Talk with the children about how all of this requires them to work as a group.

TEAHER-TO-TEACHER TIP

- Have the children practice the moves with an empty parachute first. Direct them to move the parachute up, down, fast, slow, high, low, and so on. This is a nice winter movement activity when it is too cold to play outside.

ASSESSMENT

To assess the children's learning, consider the following:
- Are the children able to follow directions to make the snowflakes dance in particular ways?
- Can the children work together successfully?

Children's Books

Millions of Snowflakes by Mary McKenna Siddals
No Two Snowflakes by Sheree Fitch
Winter's First Snowflake by Cheri L. Hallwood

Sandra Ryan, Buffalo, NY

Raking Leaves

4+

LEARNING OBJECTIVES

The children will:
1. Develop their large motor skills.
2. Learn about the autumn season.
3. Enjoy role-playing.

Materials

plastic rakes
50 or more pieces
    of red, yellow,
    brown, and
    orange scrap
    paper or tissue
    paper
masking tape
mural paper
marker
jackets for children
    to wear
work gloves
trash barrel, plastic
    laundry basket,
    or large garbage
    bag

VOCABULARY

brown   leaf   orange   pile   rake   red   yellow

PREPARATION

- Draw a large tree on the mural paper and tack it to a bulletin board with the bottom of the tree touching the floor.
- Crumple up a large number of sheets of the colored scrap paper or tissue paper.
- Disperse the "leaves" (crumpled papers) about the area beneath the tree.
- Display the jackets, work gloves, and rakes near this tree.

WHAT TO DO

1. When discussing the autumn season with the children, talk with them about what happens to the leaves and trees.
2. Show the children the tree outline on the wall, as well as the "leaves" on the ground around it.
3. Set out the jackets, plastic rakes, and other materials, and invite the children to rake up the leaves together.

TEACHER-TO-TEACHER TIP

- For extra fun, hang colored leaf shapes from the ceiling above this dramatic play area to represent falling leaves.

SONG

I'm Raking Leaves by Mary J. Murray
(Tune: "Three Blind Mice")
I'm raking leaves. I'm raking leaves.
They're falling from the trees. They're falling from the trees.
Red ones and yellow ones, orange ones and brown ones,
All kinds of colored ones. I'm raking leaves.

ASSESSMENT

To assess the children's learning, consider the following:
- Are children able to manipulate the rakes?
- Can the children work together to clean up all the leaves?

Children's Books

Apple Trees by Gail
    Saunders-Smith
Autumn Leaves Are
    Falling by Maria
    Fleming
Now It's Fall by Lois
    Lenski

Mary J. Murray, Mazomanie, WI

Throwing Snowballs

4+

LEARNING OBJECTIVES

The children will:
1. Improve their large motor skills.
2. Develop their matching and sorting skills.

Materials

12 or more white
  socks
pairs of colorful
  mittens or gloves
white mural paper
  (3' x 6' or larger)
masking tape
milk jug cap
permanent marker
basket

VOCABULARY

count   mitten   number   snow
snowball   throw   winter

PREPARATION

- Draw a simple outdoor winter scene (tree, house, snowflakes, snowperson) on the mural paper.
- Hang the mural on the wall.
- Use masking tape to mark a line about 10' from the winter scene mural.
- Roll each white sock inside of itself to create a snowball shape. Display the snowballs and mittens in a basket by the masking tape line.
- Write the numeral 1 on one side of the milk jug cap and the numeral 2 on the other side.

WHAT TO DO

1. Ask the children if they have ever played with snowballs before. Talk with the children about those experiences.
2. Tell the children they will be tossing "snowballs" at the winter scene.
3. Invite a child to flip the milk jug cap. If the cap lands with the numeral 1 facing up, ask the child to find one "snowball" and toss it at the winter scene. If the cap lands with the numeral 2 facing up, the child finds a matching pair of mittens or sock snowballs and throws both of them at the winter scene.
4. Once the children throw all the snowballs, invite the children to pile them up and repeat the activity a second time.

TEACHER TO TEACHER TIP

- Ask the children's families to donate old, clean white socks for this activity.

Children's Books

Winter by Ruth
  Thomson
The Winter Picnic by
  Robert Welber
Winter Weather by
  John Mason

ASSESSMENT

To assess the children's learning, consider the following:
- Are the children able to match like mittens or gloves?
- Can the children identify the numerals 1 and 2?

Mary J. Murray, Mazomanie, WI

Sort the Seashells

LEARNING OBJECTIVES

The children will:

1. Study an assortment of seashells and sort them by different characteristics.
2. Develop an understanding of similarities and differences.
3. Identify colors.

Materials

10–15 seashells

VOCABULARY

color   seashell   shape   size   sort   summer

PREPARATION

● Place the seashells in the math center.

WHAT TO DO

1. Engage the children in a discussion about summertime. Ask the children if they have ever visited the beach. Explain how when people visit beaches, they often see seashells in the sand and water.
2. Ask the children who have seen seashells to describe them to the rest of the children. Explain that seashells come in many different shapes, sizes, and colors.
3. Examine the seashells with the children. Talk about the different colors and shapes of the seashells. Encourage the children to hold and touch the shells. Ask questions like "What shapes do you see? Are some shells round? Pointy? Long and skinny? Are some shells bigger than others?"
4. Challenge the children to sort the shells by color, shape, size, and so on.

POEM

Seashells by Laura Wynkoop
Seashells, lovely seashells,
I found you in the sand.
I love to watch you shimmer
As I hold you in my hand.

ASSESSMENT

To assess the children's learning, consider the following:

● Can the children identify the colors of the shells?
● Are the children able to sort the shells based on a variety of characteristics?

Children's Books

Find the Seashell by Liza Alexander
Shells! Shells! Shells! by Nancy Elizabeth Wallace
What Lives in a Shell? by Kathleen Weidner Zoehfeld

Laura Wynkoop, San Dimas, CA

Counting Leaves

4+

LEARNING OBJECTIVES

The children will:
1. Become familiar with the numbers 1–5.
2. Develop their counting skills.
3. Learn to identify colors by name.

Materials

leaf outline
brown, red, yellow,
   orange, green,
   and purple
   construction
   paper
scissors (adult use
   only)

VOCABULARY

autumn	brown	fall	green	leaf
numbers 1–5	orange	purple	season	red

PREPARATION

● Make leaves using colored paper. Male one purple leaf, two green leaves, three yellow leaves, four orange leaves, and five red leaves. Write corresponding numbers on each leaf.

WHAT TO DO

1. Talk with the children about how leaves in autumn change color and fall from the trees. Ask the children if they have seen this. Ask the children what color the leaves are when they fall.
2. Show the children the leaf cutouts, and ask them to identify their colors.
3. Point out the numbers on the leaves to the children. Challenge the children to identify the numbers on the leaves.
4. Set out the leaves so the children can explore them. The children can count the number of leaves in each color, or try making patterns with the leaves.

SONG

Collecting Leaves by Kristen Peters
(Tune: "Baa, Baa Black Sheep")
Watch the leaves go floating to the ground
Yellow ones, orange ones, red, purple, brown.
Rake them into piles, jump in the leaves,
Oh, how I love the fall and the trees!
Collecting all the leaves is so much fun,
I wish I could save every single one!

Children's Books

Autumn Leaves by Ken
   Robbins
Fall Leaves by Don
   Curry
*Fletcher and the Falling
   Leaves* by Julia
   Rawlinson

ASSESSMENT

To assess the children's learning, consider the following:
● Can the children identify the colors of the leaves?
● Can the children count the numbers of leaves in each color?

Kristen Peters, Mattituck, NY

Counting Watermelon Seeds

Materials

black, pink, white,
and green
construction
paper
glue sticks
marker

LEARNING OBJECTIVES

The children will:
1. Learn that watermelons have many seeds.
2. Develop their counting skills.

VOCABULARY

fall   numbers 1–10   season   seed   summer   watermelon

PREPARATION

- Make 10 watermelon cutouts from green, white, and pink construction paper. Glue an arc of white paper on the green base, followed by a smaller arc of pink paper on top of that. Cut it in the shape of a watermelon slice.
- Write a number from 1–10 on each watermelon.
- Cut out several small black ovals to resemble watermelon seeds, or use pom-poms to stand in for the seeds.

WHAT TO DO

1. Ask the children if they have ever eaten watermelon. Ask what season they remember eating it in. Point out that watermelon is harvested in the summer, and it is a refreshing snack on hot days.
2. Show the children the watermelon and seed cutouts (or pom-poms).
3. Ask the children to identify the numbers written on each watermelon cutout.
4. Challenge the children to put the corresponding number of seeds on each watermelon cutout, counting them aloud as they do so.

POEM

Watermelon by Kristen Peters
Watery, juicy, pink, and wet.
This is the best fruit I have tasted yet!
Soft, cold slippery fun,

Chomp, chomp—what's that I bit?
Yuck! This fruit is loaded with seedy pits!

Two more bites and I'll be done.

ASSESSMENT

To assess the children's learning, consider the following:
- Can the children identify the numbers on the watermelons?
- Can the children put the corresponding number of "seeds" on each watermelon?

Children's Books

One Watermelon Seed by Celia Barker
Watermelon Day by Kathi Appelt
Watermelon Wishes by Lisa Moser

Kristen Peters, Mattituck, NY

Leaf Puzzles

4+

LEARNING OBJECTIVES

The children will:
1. Learn about the fall season.
2. Develop their math skills.

Materials

fallen leaves
scissors (adult use only)
laminator
marker

VOCABULARY

fall	leaf	numbers 1–10
part	season	whole

PREPARATION

- Collect several fallen leaves and laminate them. (Consider having the children go outside and collect some leaves for this activity.)
- Cut the laminated leaves into a number of interlocking puzzle pieces, numbering each from 1–4 or 1–10.

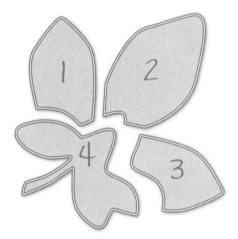

WHAT TO DO

1. Talk with the children about how, in the fall season, leaves change color and fall to the ground, and then further fall apart by breaking into several small pieces.
2. Show the children the different leaf puzzles and invite the children to explore putting them back together.
3. Challenge the children to count the number of pieces that make up each puzzle.

ASSESSMENT

To assess the children's learning, consider the following:
- Can the children put the leaf puzzles back together again?
- Can the children count the number of pieces that make up each leaf puzzle?

Cookie Zingarelli, Columbus, OH

Children's Books

Autumn by Gerda Muller
Emily's Autumn! by Janice May Udry
For the Love of Autumn by Patricia Polacco
The Pumpkin People by David Cavagnaro
The Tale of Squirrel Nutkin by Beatrix Potter

Placing Crows on the Scarecrow

4

Materials

The Little Scarecrow Boy by Margaret Wise Brown

red, blue, green, yellow, orange, purple, pink, and brown construction paper

outlines of crows and scarecrows

scissors (adult use only)

LEARNING OBJECTIVES

The children will:

1. Learn about scarecrows and farming.
2. Match colored crows to the same colored scarecrow.
3. Develop their counting and comparison skills.

VOCABULARY

crop   crow   farm   scarecrow   season

PREPARATION

- Cut out outlines of crows and scarecrows, making one scarecrow and a different number of crows in each color.
- Display the scarecrows on the wall.

WHAT TO DO

1. Gather the children together and talk to them about scarecrows. Ask the children if they have ever seen a scarecrow. Talk about what scarecrows are for, and the seasons during which people build them.
2. Read Margaret Wise Brown's *The Little Scarecrow Boy* with the children. Discuss the story with them.
3. Show the children the scarecrows on the wall. Mix up the crow cutouts and set them in front of the children. Challenge the children to identify the colors of the scarecrows and crows, and then to take turns matching them by color.
4. Challenge the children to count the number of crows in each color, and to determine which scarecrow has the most and which has the fewest crows.

SONG

Lonely Scarecrow by Kristen Peters
(Tune: "How Much Is That Doggie in the Window?")

What is that scarecrow doing in the cornfield?
He looks so sad and alone.
All the crows fly high above him.
I wish he had one of his own.

ASSESSMENT

To assess the children's learning, consider the following:

- Can the children explain the purpose of a scarecrow?
- Can the children identify the colors of the crows and scarecrows?
- Can the children say which scarecrow has the most and which has the fewest crows?

Kristen Peters, Mattituck, NY

Children's Books

Scarecrow by Cynthia Rylant
Scarecrows by Calvin Harris
Scarecrows by Lola Schaefer

Pumpkins

LEARNING OBJECTIVES

The children will:
1. Explore and describe pumpkins.
2. Learn about scales.
3. Compare their weights to that of a large pumpkin.

Materials

large pumpkin
chart paper
marker
scale

VOCABULARY

autumn	fall	heavy	less	light
more	pumpkin	season	weigh	

WHAT TO DO

1. In the fall, show the children a large pumpkin. Invite them to feel its surface and describe how it feels.
2. Ask the children to estimate how much the pumpkin weighs. Record their responses.
3. Weigh the pumpkin with the children. Ask the children if they think they weigh more or less than the pumpkin.
4. Create a two-column chart titled "Do You Weigh More or Less than a Pumpkin?"
5. Weigh the children and record their names and weights on the correct side of the column.

TEACHER-TO-TEACHER TIP

- Consider cutting the pumpkin open and cooking the pulp and using it to make pumpkin bars for a snack.

ASSESSMENT

To assess the children's learning, consider the following:
- How do the children describe the feel of the pumpkin?
- Are the children able to compare their weights to the pumpkin's?

Virginia Jean Herrod, Columbia, SC

Children's Books

Albert's Halloween: The Case of the Stolen Pumpkins by Leslie Tryon
Arthur's Halloween by Marc Brown
Arthur's Halloween Costume by Lillian Hoban
By the Light of the Halloween Moon by Caroline Stutson
Halloween Pie by Kevin O'Malley and Michael O. Tunnell

Sequencing Fall Leaves

4+

LEARNING OBJECTIVES

The children will:
1. Learn beginning sequence skills.
2. Identify and match colors and shapes.

Materials

construction paper
  or premade
  leaves, in many
  different colors
  and shapes
board for
  placement
  (optional)

VOCABULARY

| fall | leaf | orange |
| red | season | yellow |

WHAT TO DO

1. Talk with the children about the seasons, focusing on what happens to leaves in the fall.
2. Show the children the different leaves, discussing their colors and shapes.
3. Hold up a leaf and ask one child to pick another leaf that looks the same (the child can match color, shape, or both). Repeat with the other children.
4. Once the children demonstrate they are able to match, use the leaves to create a simple pattern, such as "red, yellow, red, yellow, red, yellow, red."
5. Ask a child to find the leaf that comes next in the pattern.
6. Continue with simple patterns and present challenges as appropriate.

TEACHER-TO-TEACHER TIP

* To help children remember color names, say each color name in a singsong fashion while pointing to the leaves.

Children's Books

I Am a Leaf by Jean
  Marzollo
Leaves! Leaves! Leaves!
by Nancy Elizabeth
  Wallace
Red Leaf, Yellow Leaf by
  Lois Ehlert
*We're Going on a Leaf
Hunt* by Steve Metzger

ASSESSMENT

To assess the children's learning, consider the following:
* Can the children identify the colors and describes the shapes of the leaves?
* Are the children able to match colors and shapes?
* Can the children continue a pattern with the leaves?

Sandra Ryan, Buffalo, NY

Snowball Math

4+

LEARNING OBJECTIVES

The children will:
1. Practice estimation.
2. Develop their counting skills.

Materials

cotton balls
plastic jar

VOCABULARY

count   estimate   season   snowball   winter

PREPARATION

● Place 10–20 cotton balls in the jar, and set the jar in the math center. **Note:** Vary the number of cotton balls based on the children's counting skills.

WHAT TO DO

1. Ask the children if they have ever made snowballs before. Talk about winter, snow, and games the children play in the snow.
2. Show the children the jar. Ask the children to pretend that the cotton balls are snowballs. Ask each child to estimate how many "snowballs" are in the jar. Write down the children's estimates.
3. Once each child has had a chance to respond, count the snowballs together to see whose guess was the closest.

TEACHER-TO-TEACHER TIP

● For added fun, you can use other props such as a snow hat or a toy sleigh to hold the "snowballs."

SONG

Ten Little Snowballs by Laura Wynkoop
(Tune: "Bumping Up and Down in My Little Red Wagon")
One little, two little, three little snowballs,
Four little, five little, six little snowballs,
Seven little, eight little, nine little snowballs,
Ten snowballs melting away!

Children's Books

All You Need for a Snowman by Alice Schertle
The Snowball by Jennifer Armstrong
Snowballs by Lois Ehlert

ASSESSMENT

To assess the children's learning, consider the following:
● How accurate are the children's estimates about the number of snowballs in the jar?
● Can the children count the snowballs individually?

Laura Wynkoop, San Dimas, CA

Apple and Pumpkin Count 5+

LEARNING OBJECTIVES

The children will:

1. Learn about foods that people harvest in the fall.
2. Develop their basic counting and addition skills.

Materials

construction paper
cutouts of apples
and pumpkins
(6 per item)
string
2 coat hangers

VOCABULARY

apple   autumn   fall   harvest   pumpkin   season

PREPARATION

● String three apple cutouts and three pumpkin cutouts from the coat hangers.

WHAT TO DO

1. Gather the children together. Talk with the children about how the autumn is a common time for farmers to harvest certain foods. Explain that apples and pumpkins are frequently harvested in the autumn.
2. Show the children the cutouts of the apples and pumpkins. Hang the two coat hangers from the ceiling, and attach the remaining three images of each food to the wall, or hold them up in front of the children.
3. Talk about how there are many apples and pumpkins that people harvest in the autumn, so many that it can be hard to keep track of them all.
4. Challenge the children to recite the following, counting the different number of cutouts of each food:

Apple and Pumpkin Count by Ingelore Mix

One apple there.   *One pumpkin there.*
Two apples here.   *Two pumpkins here.*
Three apples hanging   *Three pumpkins hanging*
From a chandelier.   *From a chandelier.*
How many apples?   *How many pumpkins?*

5. Some children will be able to count all the pumpkins and apples, while others will benefit from counting only those on the chandeliers or on the wall.

Children's Books

Autumn by Steven
Schnur
It's Fall! by Linda Glaser
Now It's Fall by Lois
Lenski
Ten Apples Up On Top
by Dr. Seuss

ASSESSMENT

To assess the children's learning, consider the following:

● Can the children identify the apples and pumpkins by name?
● Can the children say in which season people commonly harvest apples and pumpkins?
● Can the children count the number of apple and pumpkin cutouts?

Ingelore Mix, Amherst, NH

Calendar Toss

5+

LEARNING OBJECTIVES

The children will:
1. Begin to recognize numbers from 1–31.
2. Learn about calendars.

Materials

calendar
laminator or clear
   self-adhesive
   paper (optional)
masking tape
buttons
plastic cup

VOCABULARY

calendar   date   fall   number   spring   summer   winter

PREPARATION

- Select four pages from an old calendar. In addition to having the month's dates, each page should contain illustrations depicting one of the four seasons. Laminate for durability.
- Place the pages in an open area. Mark a line in the floor about 2' from each page with masking tape. Put a cup with 10 buttons next to the starting lines.

WHAT TO DO

1. Begin by talking with the children about the seasons. Ask the children how people identify each season. Explain that people know what season it is because of the weather, but also because people use calendars to keep track of the month and the season.
2. Show the children the pages from the calendar. Count the numbers on the calendars aloud with the children.
3. Model for the children how to toss a button onto one of the calendars, name the season and month it depicts, and then name the date on which the button landed.
4. Encourage the children to explore this activity at their own levels.

TEACHER-TO-TEACHER TIP

- For children who have trouble identifying numbers, consider simplifying the activity by having the children toss buttons and simply name the season or month of the calendar page on which they land.

ASSESSMENT

To assess the children's learning, consider the following:
- Do the children understand the basic function of calendars?
- Can the children name the seasons and months of the calendar pages?
- Can the children identify the numbers 1–31 on the calendars?

Children's Books

Calendar by Myra Cohn Livingston and Will Hillenbrand
A Child's Calendar by John Updike
Four Seasons Make a Year by Anne Rockwell
Parade Day: Marching Through the Calendar Year by Bob Barner

Susan Arentson Sharkey, El Cajon, CA

Temperature Changes

5+

LEARNING OBJECTIVES

The children will:

1. Explore changes in temperature that happen as part of seasonal changes.
2. Understand the purpose of a thermometer.
3. Learn to associate certain temperatures with hot, warm, or cold weather.
4. Learn to make and interpret a line graph.

Materials

thermometer (preferably one with large numbers that are easy to read)

monthly chart for recording the temperature each day

partially prepared line graph for the children to complete

VOCABULARY

graph   season   temperature   thermometer   weather

PREPARATION

- Place a thermometer outside the classroom so that the children can see it easily.
- Prepare two charts for recording the daily temperature, one for the last month of a season and one for the first month of the following season.
- On a sheet of poster board, make the x- and y-axes of a graph. Put dates along the x-axis and degrees of temperature along the y-axis. Leave the graph itself blank.

WHAT TO DO

1. With the children, discuss the purpose of a thermometer and how to use it. Talk about how temperatures change as the seasons change. Ask the children to describe different temperatures they have experienced at different times of the year.
2. Each day for approximately two months, invite one child to check the outdoor temperature and then record it on the monthly chart. Record the temperature each day for as long as it takes to observe a significant increase or decrease in the daily temperature.
3. At the end of the record-keeping period, show the children the blank graph, explaining what the different lines on the graph indicate.
4. Work with the children to fill in the graph. Talk with the children about what they can learn from looking at the graph.

ASSESSMENT

To assess the children's learning, consider the following:

- Can the children explain the purpose of a thermometer?
- Are the children able to mark the temperature charts?
- Do the children understand how to fill in the graph?

Children's Books

Is It Hot or Cold? Learning to Use a Thermometer by Wes Lipschultz
Temperature by Chris Woodford
Temperature by Navin Sullivan
What Is a Thermometer? by Lisa Trumbauer

Tammy Utchek Lee, Bloomingdale, IL

Weather Calendars

5+

LEARNING OBJECTIVES

The children will:

1. Learn about clouds and weather.
2. Learn about the months and seasons.
3. Develop their basic math skills.

Materials

poster board
marker

VOCABULARY

calendar   cold   hot   snowy   sunny   weather   windy

PREPARATION

● Use poster board to make one large calendar for every month of the school year.

WHAT TO DO

1. Talk with the children about the weather. Ask them what the weather has been like for the last several days.
2. Show the children the large calendars for each month. Show the children the current month's calendar. Explain the calendar to the children, and challenge them to identify the current day on the calendar.
3. Review the day's weather with the children, and then mark the calendar to indicate what the weather is like that day: sunny, rainy, windy, hot, cold, snowy?
4. Repeat this throughout each month. At the month's end, add up the number of each type of day, and talk with the children about what kinds of days are most common in the different months. Talk with the children about the general temperature of each season.

ASSESSMENT

To assess the children's learning, consider the following:

● Can the children describe what the day's weather is like?
● Can the children review the calendar to say what kind of weather was most prevalent in a given month?

Cookie Zingarelli, Columbus, OH

Children's Books

The Cloud Book by Tomie de Paola
Hi, Clouds by Carol Greene
How the Weather Works by Peter Seymour
It Looked Like Spilt Milk by Charles Green Shaw
Little Cloud by Eric Carle
Mushroom in the Rain by Mirra Ginsburg
Stormy Weather by Debi Gliori
Thunder Cake by Patricia Polacco
Today's Weather Is by Lorraine Jean Hopping

Let's Dance the Seasons!

3+

LEARNING OBJECTIVES

The children will:
1. Learn about the four seasons.
2. Develop movements that relate to each season.
3. Learn about the composer Vivaldi and his work, *Four Seasons*.

Materials

recording of Vivaldi's *Four Seasons*
stereo

VOCABULARY

composer	fall	movement	season	spring
summer	Vivaldi	weather	winter	

WHAT TO DO

1. Gather the children together. Read them a book about the seasons, as well as a book about Vivaldi (see list to the left).
2. Talk with the children about the seasons, and how the children know when the seasons change.
3. Ask the children to imagine physical ways they could indicate a particular season, such as shivering for winter cold, pounding their feet for springtime rains, making sunbeams with their arms for summer, or swaying lazily like falling leaves for fall. Encourage the children to come up with other examples. Talk about how these motions are symbols of the various seasons.
4. Play Vivaldi's *Four Seasons* and invite the children to do interpretive dances for each season.

ASSESSMENT

To assess the children's learning, consider the following:
- Can the children identify the various seasons?
- What kind of movements do the children suggest as symbols of the different seasons?
- Do the children respond to the music? Can they identify the various seasons in the music?

Donna Alice Patton, Hillsboro, OH

Children's Books

Four Seasons Make a Year by Anne Rockwell
I, Vivaldi by Janice Shefelman
The Seasons by Shannon Cannon

Maypole Dancing

4+

LEARNING OBJECTIVES

The children will:

1. Learn about colors.
2. Move their bodies to music.
3. Learn how certain cultures celebrate the coming of spring.

Materials

flower garlands
10–12 colorful
   ribbons each
   25'–30' long
tall flagpole
recordings of foot-
   tapping country
   music
stereo

VOCABULARY

festival   garland   maypole   season   spring

PREPARATION

● Ask the children to wear colorful clothes on the day of the activity.

WHAT TO DO

1. At the start of the spring season, talk with the children about maypole dances. Explain that maypole dancing is a celebration with its roots in England, and that it marks the arrival of flowers in spring.
2. Unfurl all the ribbons. Tie the ends of the ribbons halfway up the pole. Ask the children to name the colors of the ribbons they can see.
3. Start the music. Ask different children to hold the end of each ribbon and dance around the pole, weaving in and out of each other. The rest of the children then form a big circle, hold hands, and walk around the pole. As the children in the center dance, the ribbons should begin tying and knotting around the pole.
4. After a few minutes, stop the music and invite new children to hold the ribbons and dance in the center. Continue the activity until all the children have a chance to hold the ribbon and weave around the pole.
5. At the end of the activity, the pole will resemble the pattern of a woven basket. Let the children look at the pattern on the pole and take turns undoing it.

ASSESSMENT

To assess the children's learning, consider the following:

● Can the children name the colors of the ribbons tied to the pole?
● Do the children understand that maypole dances are a traditional form of welcoming the spring?

Shyamala Shanmugasundaram, Mumbai, India

Children's Books

Color Dance by Ann
   Jonas
May by Robyn Brode
*Naomi Knows It's
Springtime* by Virginia
   L. Kroll
When Will It Be Spring?
by Catherine Walters

Winter Windows

4+

LEARNING OBJECTIVES

The children will:

1. Learn to watch and copy a partner's movements.
2. Develop their observation skills.
3. Develop their small and large motor skills.

Materials

VOCABULARY

cold	mimic	mirror	partner
reflection	season	winter	

WHAT TO DO

1. In the winter, talk with the children about how they have to stay inside so much because of the cold.
2. Ask the children if they have ever looked out a window wanting to go outside and seen their reflections in the glass.
3. Invite the children to take turns going up to a classroom window and looking at their reflections. Encourage them to move around to see how their reflections mirror their movements.
4. Tell the children they will pretend to be one another's mirror reflections.
5. Separate the children into pairs. Have the children face one another. Tell one child to move around, and the other child to mirror the first child's motions.
6. After a short while, invite the children to switch positions so the first becomes the mirror of the second.

ASSESSMENT

To assess the children's learning, consider the following:

- Do the children understand what their reflections are?
- Are the children able to mimic one another's movements?

Grier Cooper, San Rafael, CA

Children's Books

EyeLike: Seasons: Change in the Natural World by PlayBac
Seasons by Blexbolex
Silly Lily and the Four Seasons by Agnes Rosenstiehl
Time and Seasons by Brenda Walpole

Snowflake Dance

4+

LEARNING OBJECTIVES

The children will:
1. Learn about snow.
2. Improve their listening skills.
3. Improve their large motor skills.

Materials

VOCABULARY

flutter   frozen   snow   snowflake
spiral   waltz   winter

WHAT TO DO

1. When the children arrive, gather them together and discuss winter weather. Ask the children if they have ever seen snow fall. Ask the children to describe what individual snowflakes look like as they fall.
2. Use words like "flutter," "spiral," and "waltz" with the children to describe snowflakes. Explain the meanings of these words to the children if they do not know them already.
3. Direct the children to compare falling snowflakes to dancing. Clap out a 3/4 waltz beat for the children to dance to.
4. Invite the children to take turns standing up and acting out a single motion that a falling snowflake makes. Ask the children to name or otherwise identify those motions.
5. Have all the children stand up together. Ask one child to name a movement snowflakes make while falling, and then have all the other children in the class make that movement.
6. Call on another child to name a movement snowflakes make while falling, and have the children make that movement.
7. Repeat until all the children have offered a movement to make.

ASSESSMENT

To assess the children's learning, consider the following:
- Can the children dance to the 3/4 beat of a waltz?
- Can the children name motions snowflakes make while falling? Can the children imitate those motions?

Kay Flowers, Summerfield, OH

Children's Books

The Snowflake by Neil Waldman
Snowflake Bentley by Jacqueline Briggs Martin
What Happens in Winter? by Sara L. Latta

Umbrella Dance

5+

LEARNING OBJECTIVES

The children will:
1. Develop their large motor skills.
2. Learn to follow directions.

Materials

music
stereo
umbrellas (1 per child)
blue paper "puddles" (1 per child)

VOCABULARY

dance   down   round   skip   twirl   under   up   walk

PREPARATION

- The day prior to doing this activity, invite the children to bring umbrellas to school.

WHAT TO DO

1. Turn on the music and invite the children to move to the music and use their umbrellas to participate in an umbrella dance.
2. Have the children spread out around the room and begin with their umbrellas closed.
3. Call out instructions for the children, such as the following:
   - Lift the umbrella over your head.
   - Point the umbrella at the sky.
   - Walk with the umbrella tip touching the ground each time you take a step.
   - Use your umbrella to make a circle in the air.
     - Walk with the umbrella over your head.
     - Set the umbrella down and dance around the umbrella.
     - Skip with your umbrella open above your head.
   - Twirl the umbrella in front of you.
   - Hold your umbrella inside the circle and walk around.
   - Set the umbrella down and lie underneath its protection.
   - Step in the puddle with one foot.
   - Walk around the puddle.
   - Sit in the puddle.
   - Jump over the puddle.

Children's Books

Ella's Umbrellas by Jennifer Lloyd
Umbrella Parade by Kathy Feczko
The Umbrella Queen by Shirin Yim Bridges

ASSESSMENT

To assess the children's learning, consider the following:
- Are the children able to listen and follow directions?
- Can the children manipulate the umbrellas?
- Do the children understand concepts such as *over, around, underneath,* and so on?

Mary J. Murray, Mazomanie, WI

Adopt a Tree

3+

LEARNING OBJECTIVES

The children will:
1. Learn how trees change with the seasons.
2. Gain increased awareness of their surroundings.
3. Develop their comparison skills.

Materials

camera

VOCABULARY

berry	change	different	flower	leaf
nut	same	tree	weather	

WHAT TO DO

1. Take the children outside for a walk, and help them to select a tree to serve as the class tree.
2. Once everyone agrees upon a tree, spend some time talking about how the tree looks. Ask, "Does it have leaves? If so, what color are they? Are there any flowers, nuts, or berries on the tree? Are there any birds or animals in the tree?"

3. Take a picture of your tree, and post it on a bulletin board where the children can look at it often.
4. Visit the tree once during each season of the year, taking a picture each time.
5. After each visit, spend some time looking at the pictures with the children. Encourage the children to discuss things that have changed and things that have stayed the same.

ASSESSMENT

To assess the children's learning, consider the following:
- Can the children describe the tree?
- Do the children note differences in the tree in different seasons?
- In which season do the children think the tree looks the best?

Erin Huffstetler , Maryville, TN

Children's Books

A Friend for All Seasons by Julia Hubery
The Seasons of Arnold's Apple Tree by Gail Gibbons
A Tree for All Seasons by Robin Bernard

Fall Nature Walk

3+

LEARNING OBJECTIVES

The children will:
1. Learn about the fall season.
2. Explore how things look outside during the fall season.
3. Develop their observational skills.
4. Develop their small motor skills.

Materials

small beanbag
paper
markers, crayons,
  colored pencils

VOCABULARY

change   fall   leaf   season   squirrel

WHAT TO DO

1. On a nice fall day, bring the children outside and go on a walk. Determine the direction of the walk by giving a child the beanbag and having the child toss it in one direction.
2. Walk with the children to the beanbag, and invite the children to look around that area and describe season-related things they see. Are squirrels burying nuts? Are leaves changing colors and falling? Write down what the children describe.
3. After the children finish describing what they see in that location, give the beanbag to another child to toss in a different direction. Go to the beanbag and repeat the process.
4. Bring the children back inside, and give them paper, markers, crayons, and so on, and invite them to make drawings of season-related things they saw while outside. Read some ideas to the children if they are not sure what to draw.
5. Hang the children's pictures in the classroom.

ASSESSMENT

To assess the children's learning, consider the following:
- Can the children describe things happening in the world that relate to the fall season?
- Can the children recall things they saw outside when they come back inside?
- What fall-related images are the children drawing?

Cookie Zingarelli, Columbus, OH

Children's Books

Fun with Nature by Mel Boring
It's Autumn! by Noemi Weygant
It's Fall by Linda Glaser
Marmalade's Yellow Leaf by Cindy Wheeler
The Tale of Squirrel Nutkin by Beatrix Potter

Sweet Pea Teepee in Spring

Materials

sweet pea seeds
   from a packet
8–10 straight sticks,
   all 5'–6' tall
small shovels
fertilizer
twine

LEARNING OBJECTIVES

The children will:
1. Participate in the hands-on experience of planting.
2. Develop an appreciation for gardening.
3. Improve their small and large motor skills.

VOCABULARY

garden   season   spring   sweet pea   teepee   weather

WHAT TO DO

1. On a nice spring day, show the children the materials and then take them outside to a designated area, such as a garden at the preschool. Explain that the children will be planting seeds to make a sweet pea teepee.
2. Place three of the sticks in the ground and tie them together at the top with twine, forming a tripod.
3. Add the other sticks until they all come together at the top. Tie them together.
4. Make sure the sticks are stable enough to support climbing plants. Be sure to leave a "doorway" into the teepee.
5. Help the children prepare the soil around the base of the sticks by adding the right amount of water. Add fertilizer if necessary.
6. Dig small holes and plant the seeds at the base of the sticks.
7. Check the teepee each school day and water as needed.
8. The plants will sprout and begin to climb the sticks. Some of the vines may need to be wrapped around a stick.
9. Within a few weeks, the sweet pea teepee will be a nice place for the children to visit. Once the plants reach the top of the sticks, take a picture of each child in the "doorway" and send these photos home with the children.

Children's Books

The Curious Garden by Peter Brown
Flower Garden by Eve Bunting
Jack's Garden by Henry Cole
My Garden by Kevin Henkes

ASSESSMENT

To assess the children's learning, consider the following:
● Do the children understand how plants grow in soil?
● Are the children all able to participate in this project?

Shirley Anne Ramaley, Sun City, AZ

Fun at the Seashore

3+

LEARNING OBJECTIVES

The children will:

1. Explore different textures.
2. Learn how to pack wet sand to make free-standing structures.
3. Develop their large motor skills.

Materials

various types of
    seashells/sea
    objects
sand table or
    sandbox
plastic condiment
    squeeze bottles
plastic cups

VOCABULARY

dribble   moisten   pack   sand   summer   texture

PREPARATION

- Fill clean condiment squeeze bottles with clean water.

WHAT TO DO

1. Talk with the children about what they do during the summer. Ask the children if they have ever been to the beach during the summer.
2. Ask the children to gather around the sand table. Talk about how people at the beach in the summertime often play with sand.
3. Show the children how to carefully dribble water on dry sand to moisten it, pack the wet sand into a plastic cup or seashell, and turn it over to make a standing structure.
4. As the children play and explore, encourage them to feel the textures of wet and dry sand, as well as the hard and smooth or rough and bumpy textures of the seashells and sea objects.
5. Call attention to the difference between wet and dry sand textures. Point out to the children how dribbling water on dry sand changes the texture and makes it easier to pack.
6. Encourage experimentation. Challenge the children to make a seashell stick to the side of a sand structure, or to try stacking one structure on top of another.

TEACHER-TO-TEACHER TIP

- Include some math in this activity by counting the cups full of wet sand the children use to make their structures or how many seashells they include in a design.

Children's Books

On the Seashore by
Anna Milbourne
The Seashore Book by
Charlotte Zolotow
A Walk on the Beach by
Jo Waters

ASSESSMENT

To assess the children's learning, consider the following:

- Do the children build structures with sand and water?
- Do the children comment on the texture of the sand and shells?

Kay Flowers, Summerfield, OH

Summer Sandcastles

4+

Materials

sand and water
   table
pails in various
   shapes and sizes
shovels
seashells

LEARNING OBJECTIVES

The children will:

1. Use tools to build sandcastles in the sand table.
2. Develop small and large motor skills.
3. Develop sharing and cooperative play skills.

VOCABULARY

sand   beach   sandcastle   shovel   pail   seashell

PREPARATION

● Make sure the table is filled with sand and fresh water. Sprinkle seashells in the sand.

WHAT TO DO

1. Ask the children if they have ever made sandcastles at the beach.
2. Discuss the children's experiences, and ask what they used to make their sandcastles.
3. Show the children the materials at the sand and water table. Encourage the children to pretend that the sand and water table is a beach. Have them use shovels and pails to build sandcastles. They can use the seashells to decorate their sandcastles.

TEACHER-TO-TEACHER TIP

● Spread beach towels on the floor around the sand and water table. This will keep the floor clean and add a fun atmosphere.

POEM

A Grand Castle by Laura Wynkoop
Let's go to the beach, it's a bright summer day!
Let's play by the water for hours.
We'll make a grand castle from water and sand
With a drawbridge and lots of tall towers.

ASSESSMENT

To assess the children's learning, consider the following:

● Are the children able to use tools to build sandcastles?
● Can the children describe what they enjoy about sandcastles?

Children's Books

The Sandcastle by M.P. Robertson
The Sandcastle Contest by Robert Munsch
Watch Me Build a Sandcastle by Jack Otten

Laura Wynkoop, San Dimas, CA

Fall Color Changes

4+

LEARNING OBJECTIVES

The children will:
1. Learn about the color changes of leaves in the fall.
2. Learn that some trees change colors and others do not.
3. Develop their small motor skills.

Materials

construction paper
    in various colors
child-safe scissors
pictures from
    magazines of fall
    colors
paste

VOCABULARY

change	deciduous	evergreen	fall
leaf	orange	red	yellow

WHAT TO DO

1. With the children, discuss how some trees change in the fall. Talk about how evergreen trees do not change color and how deciduous trees do change color.
2. If the children live in an area where leaves change, talk about those trees. Encourage the children to talk about the trees in their neighborhoods. Have they seen any color changes?
3. At the tables, set out the materials and invite the children to cut out leaves in fall colors, using colored construction paper. (**Note:** Consider cutting out some samples for the children to follow.) The children can also cut pictures from magazines.
4. Have the children paste their cutouts on plain construction or poster paper to make a collage.

POEM

Fall Colors by Shirley Anne Ramaley
Orange, brown, yellow, and red,
Leaves are falling all around.
Everywhere I look I see
Many colors on the ground.

ASSESSMENT

To assess the children's learning, consider the following:
* Can the children name the colors that leaves turn?
* Do the children understand that some trees change colors while others do not?
* Are the children able to create leaves or cut out images of leaves?

Shirley Anne Ramaley, Sun City, AZ

Children's Books

Investigating Why Leaves Change Their Color by Ellen Rene
Scholastic Science Readers: Fall Leaves Change Color by Kathleen Weidner Zoehfeld
Why Do Leaves Change Color? by Betsy Maestro

From Caterpillar to Butterfly

4+

LEARNING OBJECTIVES

The children will:

1. Learn about the process of butterflies coming out of cocoons.
2. Develop their observation skills.

Materials

glass jar
milkweed leaf
small stick
gauze
butterfly egg
paper
markers, crayons,
   pencils

VOCABULARY

butterfly   cocoon   larva   migration   nectar

PREPARATION

● Purchase butterfly eggs prior to this activity.

WHAT TO DO

1. Engage the children in a discussion about butterflies, and how they are spring-time and summertime creatures. Ask where the children have seen butterflies, what time of year it was, and what the butterflies were doing.
2. Explain to the children how butterflies come from caterpillars.
3. Tell the children they will be helping to raise a butterfly from an egg to full growth. Invite the children to make sketches and drawings during each step of the process.
4. Show the children the glass jar. Place the butterfly egg, milkweed leaf, and small stick inside the jar for the children to see. **Note:** Make sure the leaf remains moist, though not very wet.
5. Once the caterpillar emerges, cover the jar with a piece of gauze. The caterpillar will need replenished milkweed leaves over time.
6. Eventually, the caterpillar should attach to the stick and form a cocoon. Show this to the children and discuss what they see.
7. Eventually the butterfly will emerge from the cocoon. When this happens, take the jar outside with the children and remove the gauze so the butterfly can go free.
8. After the butterfly is gone, talk with the children about each step in the process. Encourage them to review their drawings as they discuss what happened.

Children's Books

Charlie the Caterpillar by Dom Deluise
Clara Caterpillar by Pamela Duncan Edwards
Nature's Children: Monarch Butterfly by Bill Ivy
The Very Hungry Caterpillar by Eric Carle

ASSESSMENT

To assess the children's learning, consider the following:

● Do the children understand that caterpillars become butterflies?
● Are the children engaged and interested in the process? What kinds of illustrations do they make?

Ingelore Mix, Amherst, NH

Icy Explorations

4+

LEARNING OBJECTIVES

The children will:

1. Identify and label materials.
2. Observe and describe experiences.
3. Develop their fine motor skills.
4. Learn about colors.

Materials

small plastic winter
    animals: polar
    bears, seals,
    penguins, and so
    on
small containers
tongue depressors
salt shakers
eyedroppers
colored water

VOCABULARY

| cold | freezing | iceberg | melting |
| temperature | snow | winter | |

PREPARATION

- Place plastic winter animals in each small container, and then pour in water to fill the container.
- Create a mini iceberg by placing the filled containers in the freezer until the water freezes.
- Set out the small jars with colored water.

WHAT TO DO

1. Talk with the children about the winter season and how cold it gets. Ask the children if they have ever seen a block of ice floating in a creek, river, or lake. Explain that these are called icebergs.
2. Provide each child with an iceberg. Ask the children what they know about icebergs.
3. Demonstrate how to use the eyedroppers in the colored water: Challenge the children to predict what will happen when the iceberg and the colored water meet. Drop the colored water onto the iceberg and observe what happens to the iceberg.
4. Shake some salt from the salt shaker onto the colored iceberg and stir the mixture with a tongue depressor.
5. Continue this procedure until the ice melts away and the plastic animal is found.
6. Talk with the children about what is happening to the iceberg. Ask if this matches the children's predictions.

ASSESSMENT

To assess the children's learning, consider the following:

- Can the children describe what is happening to the iceberg and why?
- Are the children able to follow the directions?

Children's Books

First Snow by Bernette
    G. Ford
The Hat by Jan Brett
The Mitten by Jan Brett
Sadie and the Snowman
    by Allen Morgan
The Snowy Day by Ezra
    Jack Keats
When Winter Comes by
    Robert Maass
*White Snow, Bright
    Snow* by Alvin R.
    Tresselt

Kaethe Lewandowski, Centreville, VA

The Robin Redbreast

4+

LEARNING OBJECTIVES

The children will:

1. Learn about how birds make their nests in spring.
2. Learn about birds' eggs and chicks.

Materials

paper strips
strings
twigs
ribbons
blue paper
scissors (adult use
   only)

VOCABULARY

bird   egg   hatch   nest   spring   twig

PREPARATION

● From blue paper cut out three egg shapes.

WHAT TO DO

1. Show the children the paper strips, strings, and other materials. Explain that these are some of the kinds of materials birds use to make their nests.
2. Choose one child to be the robin redbreast. Spread the nesting materials outside the circle of children.
3. Invite the children to sing the following song, while the "robin" goes around them, gathering the nesting material and building a nest inside the circle.

Robin's Nest by Ingelore Mix
(Tune: "London Bridge Is Falling Down")

Robin collects lots of stuff,
Lots of stuff, lots of stuff,
Robin collects lots of stuff,
Until she has enough.

For her chicks she builds a nest,
Builds a nest, builds a nest.
For her chicks she builds a nest.
She builds the very best.

Deep inside she lays her eggs,
Lays her eggs, lays her eggs.
Deep inside she lays her eggs
In the nest she's made.

We wait and wait and wait
*   some more,*
Wait some more, wait some more.
We wait and wait and wait
*   some more,*
Knowing what's in store.

And then we see three chicks
*   pop out,*
Chicks pop out, chicks pop out.
And then we see three chicks
*   pop out*
To greet the morning sun.

Children's Books

Birds by Kevin Henkes
Birds, Nests & Eggs by
   Mel Boring
Grumpy Bird by Jeremy
   Tankard

ASSESSMENT

To assess the children's learning, consider the following:

● Do the children know the birds come back in the spring?
● Can the children describe the process through which birds hatch their eggs?

Ingelore Mix, Amherst, NH

Winter Tracks

LEARNING OBJECTIVES

The children will:

1. Learn about animals that live through snowy conditions.
2. Learn that animals have distinct types of footprints.
3. Develop their small motor skills.

Materials

images of winter
  animals (deer,
  bird, bunny,
  raccoon, mouse)
  and their tracks
cotton
construction paper
  in various colors
markers
child-safe scissors

VOCABULARY

footprint   season   snow   track   winter

PREPARATION

● Scatter some cotton balls around on the floor, like snow. Hide the pictures of animals in different parts of the classroom, putting down images of their tracks in lines through the cotton "snow" toward their locations.

WHAT TO DO

1. Gather the children together and talk with them about the winter. Ask the children what kind of animals they have seen outdoors in the winter.
2. Read the children a book about animals in the winter (see list to the left).
3. Point out the animal tracks on the floor. Ask the children if they recognize any of the footprints in the "snow."
4. Invite the children to follow the tracks and see whether they correctly identified the animals who left the tracks.
5. Set out the markers, paper, and child-safe scissors. Show the children how to draw outlines of their footprints and then cut them out. Help the children make tracks of themselves through the classroom.

SONG

Winter Tracks by Kristen Peters
(Tune: "Baa, Baa Black Sheep")
Follow the tracks in the white, wet snow.
Uphill, downhill, wherever they may go.
Big tracks, little tracks; wonder who made them,
Leading under a bush or into a den.
Follow the tracks and maybe we will see
What animal is hiding. Who could it be?

Children's Books

Footprints in the Snow
  by Cynthia Benjamin
Snow by Cynthia Rylant
Tracks in the Snow by
  Wong Herbert Yee

ASSESSMENT

To assess the children's learning, consider the following:

● Can the children name the animals that made the tracks in the snow?
● Are the children able to trace and cut out their own shoe prints?

Kristen Peters, Mattituck, NY

Frog Jump

5+

LEARNING OBJECTIVES

The children will:
1. Learn about the process by which frogs develop.
2. Develop their large motor skills.

Materials

pictures of stages in the frog life cycle
large sheets of heavy green paper or card stock
scissors (adult use only)
giant foam or rubber dice or number cards

VOCABULARY

amphibian   growth   frog   season   spring   tadpole

PREPARATION

- Find images (from books, magazines, or the Internet) of the following:
  - frog spawn
  - tadpole with short tail
  - tadpole with long tail
  - tadpole with long tail and short legs
  - tadpole with four limbs and shorter tail
  - small frog
  - medium-sized frog
  - large frog
- Cut out huge lily pads from green paper and arrange these throughout the classroom about four to six child-size jumps apart. Attach a picture of a frog's life stage to each lily pad.

WHAT TO DO

1. Talk with the children about how in the springtime new young creatures begin to grow. Show the children images of the frog's life cycle.
2. Show the children the "lily pads" set up around the classroom.
3. Starting at the frog spawn lily pad, have the children take turns throwing the dice and doing as many squatting frog jumps or hops toward the next lily pad as the dice allow.
4. When the children reach each lily pad, they look at the image attached to it and name the frog's stage of development.

ASSESSMENT

To assess the children's learning, consider the following:
- Do the children understand the basic life cycle of a frog?
- Are the children able to identify the frog's life stages by looking at the cards on the lily pads?
- Are the children able to frog-hop from lily pad to lily pad?

Anne Adeney, Plymouth, United Kingdom

Children's Books

Frog and Toad Are Friends by Arnold Lobel
Frog on His Own by Mercer Mayer
Frogs by Gail Gibbons
Jump, Frog, Jump! by Robert Kalan

Learning About Spring, Summer, Fall, and Winter

5

LEARNING OBJECTIVES

The children will:
1. Learn how to identify the seasonal characteristics.
2. Learn how weather, animal behavior, plants, trees, and outdoor activities change with the seasons.

Materials

large calendar
poster for each
   season
drawing paper
crayons
copies of children's
   books listed
   below

VOCABULARY

autumn   fall   spring   summer   winter

WHAT TO DO

1. Divide the children into four groups with a season poster displayed for each group.
2. Talk about what various plants and animals do in the different seasons.
3. On one or several large sheets of paper, make a circle with the names of each season written at equal distances around it.

Winter

Spring

4. Provide the children with paper, markers, crayons, and so on, and invite them to draw pictures that remind them of the seasons.
5. Talk with the children as they work. Help them label their pictures, either with their own names or with the names of what they are drawing.
6. Attach the children's images in the appropriate locations on the large season circle.

ASSESSMENT

To assess the children's learning, consider the following:
- Can the children identify what makes the various seasons different?
- Can the children explain what various animals and plants do in the different seasons?
- What kinds of seasonal images are the children creating?

Children's Books

It's Fall by Linda Glaser
It's Spring by Linda Glaser
It's Summer by Linda Glaser
It's Winter by Linda Glaser

Annie Laura Smith, Huntsville, AL

Summer in the Desert

LEARNING OBJECTIVES

The children will:

1. Learn about cacti and understand they are succulents.
2. Understand how desert plants store water.
3. Learn about plant life in the desert in summer.
4. Develop their small motor skills.

Materials

magazine pictures
   of the desert and
   cacti
crayons
construction paper
child-safe scissors
paste or glue

VOCABULARY

cactus	desert	drought	saguaro
spine	succulent	weather	

WHAT TO DO

1. Read the children a book about the desert climate (see the list to the left for suggestions) and then engage the children in a discussion about desert plants.
2. Talk about succulents and the fact that all cacti are succulents, but not all succulents are cacti.
3. Show the children the materials. Invite the children to cut out pictures of cacti and paste them onto construction paper, making a collage of their choosing. Also encourage the children to draw and color cacti.
4. When finished, help the children sign their names and put the children's papers on the wall for the children's parents and family members to see.

TEACHER-TO-TEACHER TIP

- Children who don't live in the American Southwest may not understand that there is little rain during the summer.

ASSESSMENT

To assess the children's learning, consider the following:

- Do the children understand that cacti prepare for the hot summer by storing water?
- Can the children identify which plants are cacti and which are not?

Shirley Anne Ramaley, Sun City, AZ

Children's Books

Cactus Desert by Donald Silver and Patricia Wynne
A Desert Habitat by Kelley MacAulay and Bobbie Kalman
Deserts by Gail Gibbons
Here Is the Southwestern Desert by Madeleine Dunphy and Anne Coe
Way Out in the Desert by T.J. Marsh

Autumn Apples

3+

LEARNING OBJECTIVES

The children will:

1. Learn about apples.
2. Identify colors.
3. Taste different types of apples.

Materials

apples (several
different
varieties)
knife (adult use
only)
cutting board
napkins or small
paper plates

VOCABULARY

apple   autumn   fall   green   pink   red   yellow

PREPARATION

● Display the apples in the snack and cooking area.

WHAT TO DO

1. Tell the children that many different kinds of apples ripen in the fall. Apples can be red, pink, yellow, or green depending on their type. An apple can even be more than one color, like a Pink Lady that is pink and yellow, or a McIntosh that is red and green.
2. Ask the children to identify the colors of the apples in the snack center.
3. Use the knife and cutting board to slice the apples. Place the apple slices on napkins or small paper plates, and pass them out to the children.
4. Ask the children to describe the taste and texture of the different kinds of apples. "Are some sweet? Tart? Crunchy? Soft?" Help the children think of words to describe their apples slices.

TEACHER-TO-TEACHER TIP

● Keep the knife and cutting board in a secure location when not in use. Remind the children that the knife is for adult use only.

ASSESSMENT

To assess the children's learning, consider the following:

● Are the children able to identify the colors of the apples?
● Can the children use one or two words to describe the taste or texture of their apple slices?

Laura Wynkoop, San Dimas, CA

Children's Books

Apple Seasons by Gail
Gibbons
Apples, Apples by
Kathleen Weidner
Zoehfeld
*One Little, Two Little,
Three Little Apples* by
Matt Ringler

Autumn Applesauce

3+

LEARNING OBJECTIVES

The children will:
1. Learn how apples are commonly harvested in the fall.
2. Learn to understand a process.
3. Help make applesauce.

Materials

applesauce recipe
  (see to the right)
saucepan
oven
potato masher
plates
spoons

VOCABULARY

apple   autumn   fall   harvest   prepare   season

RECIPE

4 Cortland apples
¾ cup water
¼ cup brown sugar
½ teaspoon cinnamon
(Double the recipe for larger groups of children.)

PREPARATION

● Core the apples. Place all the ingredients in a saucepan. Cover and cook for 20 minutes just prior to doing this activity. Stir occasionally as mixture cooks. Let cool before showing the mixture to the children.

WHAT TO DO

1. Ask the children if they have ever eaten applesauce. Explain that applesauce is made from cooked, mashed apples. Talk with the children about how farmers commonly harvest apples in the fall.
2. Show the children a second set of unmixed ingredients and tell them they will be making applesauce together.
3. Show the children the ingredients mixed and heated in the saucepan. **Note:** Be sure the saucepan and contents are cool before placing them within the children's reach.
4. Give each child the potato masher in turn, and let each child mash the mixture in the saucepan.
5. After the children thoroughly mash the mixture, stir it a little, and serve it to the children on individual plates.
6. Talk with the children about how they helped to make applesauce.

Children's Books

Autumn by Steven Schnur
It's Fall! by Linda Glaser
Ten Apples Up On Top by Dr. Seuss

ASSESSMENT

● Do the children understand that making applesauce is a process?
● Do the children enjoy their snack? Are the children proud to have helped make their food?

Ingelore Mix, Amherst, NH

Season's Eating!

3+

LEARNING OBJECTIVES

The children will:

1. Learn about the seasons.
2. Learn to associate certain symbols with each season.

Materials

slice and bake
   cookie dough
cookie cutters—
   leaves,
   pumpkins,
   snowflakes,
   tulips, and other
   seasonal shapes
waxed paper sheet
   per child—large
   enough to
   completely cover
   cookie dough
   (child will press
   dough flat inside
   the waxed paper)
stove or toaster
   oven to bake
   cookies
plastic baggies

Children's Books

Every Season by Shelley
Rotner and Anne Love
   Woodhull
Seasons by Claire
   Llewellyn
*The Seasons of Arnold's
Apple Tree* by Gail
   Gibbons

VOCABULARY

fall   season   spring   summer   weather   winter

PREPARATION

- Knead the cookie dough into fist-sized balls, making one per child.
- Roll the balls in waxed paper, and slide each wrapped ball of dough into its own plastic baggie.
- Write each child's name on one baggie.

WHAT TO DO

1. Read books about the seasons with the children (see list at the left). Discuss the symbols that indicate each season.
2. Show the children the materials. Give each child a ball of cookie dough wrapped completely in waxed paper.
3. Invite the children to press their dough as flat as possible.
4. Pass out seasonal cookie cutters the children can use to make seasonal cookie shapes. Talk with the children about the shapes they choose. Ask why they picked one seasonal shape over another.
5. Put the cookies in the oven and bake them (adult only step). When they are cool, serve the cookies.

TEACHER-TO-TEACHER TIP

- Consider making a graph of the seasonal cookies to determine which symbols and seasons were the most popular.

ASSESSMENT

To assess the children's learning, consider the following:

- Do children recognize certain symbols as associated with specific seasons?
- Do children understand the concept of differing seasons?
- Can the children talk about why they picked certain cookie-cutter symbols?

Donna Alice Patton, Hillsboro, OH

Taste the Seasons

3+

LEARNING OBJECTIVES

The children will:

1. Learn that each season produces special foods.
2. Explore the tastes, colors, and textures of a variety of seasonal foods.

Materials

foods from each season

VOCABULARY

farmer	fresh	harvest
pick	seasonal	various food names

PREPARATION

- Select foods that are in season in the summer, winter, spring, and fall.
- Chop the foods into sample sizes.
- Set out each season's selections on separate trays and cover the trays with cloth.

WHAT TO DO

1. Talk with the children about how certain foods grow in particular seasons. Ask the children if they can name foods that are connected with a particular season.
2. Lift the cover off of the summer tray, and explain that farmers harvest these foods in the summer.
3. Invite the children to try the foods on the tray. Talk with them about the flavors of the foods.
4. Repeat the process until the children taste and discuss all the foods on each tray.

ASSESSMENT

To assess the children's learning, consider the following:

- Can the children say what foods farmers harvest in particular seasons?
- Can the children talk about which foods they liked the most or the least?

Erin Huffstetler, Maryville, TN

Children's Books

Applesauce Season by Eden Ross Lipson
Maple Syrup Season by Ann Purmell
An Orange in January by Dianna Hutts Aston

Like the Breezes of the Seasons

3+

LEARNING OBJECTIVES

The children will:
1. Learn about the different seasons.
2. Move like the wind during different seasons.
3. Follow directions.

Materials

VOCABULARY

breeze	brisk	fall	gust
season	spring	summer	winter

WHAT TO DO

1. As the children move from one area to another during the day, direct them to move how the wind blows during the different seasons. Choose different movements from below for different times of the day.

    - Move like the breeze in the summer, cool in the heat (put arms out to the side and sway side to side while walking).
    - Move like the wind in the fall, tumbling the leaves (hold arms up and then flutter hands down like leaves, repeating while walking).
    - Move like the brisk gust in the winter, cold and mean (swing arms at sides quickly and put on stern faces).
    - Move like the wind in the spring, through long grass green (hold arms up while walking, waving them back and forth like grass).

TEACHER-TO-TEACHER TIP

- For transitions while children are waiting in line, or to fill in a short gap between activities in the classroom, combine all four seasons into a single poem and allow children to act them out as you narrate.

ASSESSMENT

To assess the children's learning, consider the following:
- Do the children understand the differences between the seasons?
- Can the children make the motions as described?

Children's Books

Feel the Wind by Arthur Dorros
Like a Windy Day by Frank Asch
The Wind Blew by Pat Hutchins

Sarah Stasik, Bent Mountain, VA

Activity Index by Season

Index of Children's Books

Index